BECOMING DIGITAL

Toward a Post-Internet Society

BECOMING DIGITAL

Toward a Post-Internet Society

BY

VINCENT MOSCO
Queen's University

United Kingdom — North America — Japan
India — Malaysia — China

Emerald Publishing Limited
Howard House, Wagon Lane, Bingley BD16 1WA, UK

First edition 2017

Copyright © 2017 Emerald Publishing Limited

Reprints and permissions service
Contact: permissions@emeraldinsight.com

British Library Cataloguing in Publication Data
A catalogue record for this book is available from the British
Library

ISBN: 978-1-78743-296-3 (Print)
ISBN: 978-1-78743-295-6 (Online)
ISBN: 978-1-78743-675-6 (Epub)

ISOQAR certified
Management System,
awarded to Emerald
for adherence to
Environmental
standard
ISO 14001:2004.

Certificate Number 1985
ISO 14001

INVESTOR IN PEOPLE

For Noelle

CONTENTS

List of Tables   ix

About the Author   xi

Preface   xiii

1. The Next Internet   1

2. Converging Technologies   15

3. Power, Politics and Political Economy   57

4. The Body and Culture   97

5. Problems   129

6. Citizenship in a Post-Internet World   175

Endnotes   213

Further Reading   221

Index   223

LIST OF TABLES

Chapter 2

Table 1   Forecast Growth in the Number of
Internet of Things Devices (in
Billions)..   44

Chapter 3

Table 2   The Five Largest Firms in the
World by Market Value in
$Billions US.   65

Chapter 5

Table 3   A Partial List of Data Facebook
and Its Advertisers Gather
about Users..   163

ABOUT THE AUTHOR

Vincent Mosco is Professor Emeritus, Queen's University, Canada where he held the Canada Research Chair in Communication and Society. He is also Distinguished Professor, New Media Centre, School of Journalism and Communication, Fudan University, Shanghai. Dr. Mosco completed the B.A. at Georgetown (Summa Cum Laude, 1970) and received the Ph.D. in Sociology from Harvard in 1975.

Dr. Mosco is author or editor of 23 books and over 200 articles and book chapters on communication, technology, and society including *The Digital Sublime* and *The Political Economy of Communication*. His *To the Cloud: Big Data in a Turbulent World* was named a 2014 Outstanding Academic Title by Choice: Current Reviews for Academic Libraries.

Dr. Mosco serves on the editorial boards of academic journals throughout the world and has held research positions in the U.S. government with the White House Office of Telecommunication Policy, the National Research Council and the U.S. Congress Office of Technology Assessment and in Canada with the Ministry of Communication. He was a long-time research associate of the Harvard University Program on Information Resources Policy. In 2004 Dr. Mosco received the Dallas W. Smythe Award for outstanding achievement in communication research. *The Digital*

Sublime won the 2005 Olson Award for outstanding book in the field of rhetoric and cultural studies. In 2014, the Association for Education in Journalism and Mass Communication honoured Dr. Mosco and his partner in life and in research, Dr. Catherine McKercher, with the Professional Freedom and Responsibility Award for outstanding achievement in research and activism.

PREFACE

When you write, you illuminate what's hidden, and that's a political act.

— Grace Paley

Grace Paley was a great American storyteller, primarily a short story writer whose work was celebrated by critics and fellow writers alike. The consummate New Yorker, she wrote from her home in 1950s Greenwich Village about the lives of working class women, especially the daughters of immigrant families, who displayed courage and humor as they struggled to build a life of their own. Unlike Virginia Woolf, who sought a room of her own, Paley was most comfortable writing at the kitchen table amid the hubbub of life in a lower Manhattan apartment. While well recognized, her writing did not receive the credit it deserved. She was a woman working in a male-dominated field and she was a political activist who rarely passed up a progressive cause. But mainly, it was because Paley's political sensibility infused the everyday lives of her characters. If only, critics said, she would spend more time honing her craft. By this they meant: spend less time on the picket line and focus more on the transcendent and less political dimensions of life. Paley's response was that all writing is political in the deep sense of uncovering the less visible features of life.

This sensibility provides inspiration for *Becoming Digital*. It too is political in the sense that the book uncovers aspects of the digital world, which, if not hidden, receive too little public attention. Having grown my own roots in the same Manhattan neighbourhoods that Paley lived in and wrote strengthens my feeling of connection, as does the choice to write every word in the kitchens and other busy spaces that fill my everyday life.

Becoming Digital builds on my 2014 book *To the Cloud*, which identified some of the early steps leading to what *Becoming Digital* calls the Next Internet. Specifically, it provides a brief examination of today's leap into the online world by analyzing the social, political, economic, and cultural consequences of Cloud Computing, Big Data Analytics, and the Internet of Things, which are converging to create global networks of unprecedented power. It does not claim to be an exhaustive treatment. There are many excellent books that provide in-depth treatment of specific pieces of the Next Internet puzzle, several of which are identified at the end of the book. Rather, *Becoming Digital* offers a summary overview for those who want to learn about the digital world and its emerging challenges and potential solutions. Specifically, it is a guide to the central features of the Next Internet, including the technologies that power it, the institutions that shape it, the problems it creates, and the potential steps forward that might enable a genuinely democratic Next Internet. By this I mean a digital world that guarantees open access to all citizens and opportunities to use the network to build a better world.

I am grateful to many people for helping to make this book possible. I would like to single out a few for special thanks. Professor Isaac Serfaty-Nahon kindly invited me to give the opening address at the launch of a new Ph.D. program in Communication at the University of Ottawa. The speech afforded me the opportunity to speak about the central themes of this book and the long period of audience questions and comments were enormously helpful. Thank you Professor Serfaty-Nahon and all of your colleagues and students.

For more than a decade, it has been my pleasure to work with Professor Cao Jin of Fudan University, Shanghai on numerous research and education projects. Over the years I have come to appreciate her extraordinary skill as a scholar, teacher and creative administrator. I am especially grateful for the opportunity she provided to lecture about the Next Internet in Shanghai and Chengdu in the summer of 2016. As always, you, your students and your colleagues provided a warm welcome, a receptive audience, and valuable insights that were most useful in writing this book.

I would also like to express my deep appreciation to David Flanagan, a fellow member of the Regis High School class of 1966, who kindly invited me to lecture on the Next Internet at the 50th reunion of our class. Regis High School is a Jesuit institution in Manhattan that, thanks to a generous donor, provides an extraordinary free education worth far more than my family, and the families of most of my class-mates, could ever afford. Throughout my life, I have appreciated its commitment to a rigorous classical education and to social justice.

Thank you to my dear friend and former student Dr. Ian Nagy for your careful reading of the entire manuscript and to my daughter Rosemary Mosco who took time out from her own writing and activism to offer suggestions that enriched a chapter on what it means to be a citizen in a digital world.

Life is a mystery and no more so than in the deaths that bring great sadness and the births that provide unrestrained joy. Over the course of 12 months from early 2016 to the start of 2017, I lost three former students who had built successful careers as critical communication scholars and teachers. Professor Vanda Rideout was a senior sociologist at the University of New Brunswick in Canada where she was an accomplished scholar, beloved by her students, and a leader among her colleagues. I supervised Vanda through completion of her M.A. and Ph.D. degrees. She also served as a research assistant for the 1996 edition of my book *The Political Economy of Communication* and we published articles together. In addition to producing excellent work on labour and policy formation in the digital world, she was my dear friend.

Professor Gerald Coulter was a senior sociologist at Bishop's University in Quebec where he was head of the department and a leader in cultural sociology, focusing on the work of Jean Baudrillard. As with Vanda, I had the pleasure of supervising Gerry's M.A. thesis and doctoral dissertation. His sense of humor helped ease my transition from the United States to Canada in the mid-1980s and his commitment to strong scholarship led me to appreciate the excellence of graduate students in my adopted country.

Professor Mahmoud Eid was a senior communication professor at the University of Ottawa. I taught Eid at Carleton University in the 1990s and, from the start, he impressed me with his knowledge of quantitative methodology and his commitment to address the major issues facing Muslim Canadians. The last time I saw Eid was at my University of Ottawa lecture on the Next Internet. He approached me with the dignity and generosity that masked the tensions that Muslim scholars working on issues around radicalization invariably face. He left behind a loving family and a career that ended far too soon.

I am eternally grateful for having students like Professors Rideout, Coulter and Eid. I am also blessed that in a year marked by their passing, I received the wonderful gift of a first grandchild, Noelle Rose Morton. Much of this book was written between hours spent pushing a stroller around the lakes of Orlando, Florida and doing what I could to live up to the reputation of Goofy Grandpa. Her arrival certainly eased the stresses that typically accompany the writing process. I can only hope that when she is old enough to make full use of the Next Internet, it is an open, democratic and universally accessible network that will help her work on the problems that her generation will undoubtedly face.

CHAPTER 1

THE NEXT INTERNET

What can really be contributed is not resolution but perhaps, at times, just that extra edge of consciousness.

— Raymond Williams

HAPPY BIRTHDAY INTERNET

On March 12, 2014, Google called on the world to celebrate the twenty-fifth anniversary of the Internet. It was born, in the company's view, when the computer scientist Tim Berners-Lee circulated a paper modestly called "Information Management: A Proposal" to his colleagues at CERN, the European Organization for Nuclear Research, in Geneva. The institution held vast stores of information in numerous locations and the proposal offered a model for making it accessible to any computer by connecting data sets through a series of links. Berners-Lee's paper led to the World Wide Web and eventually the Internet. Although the earliest Internet communication dated back to 1969, only those few with advanced technical skills were able to use it in the first 20 or so years.

Like many others, I did not log on until the early 1990s when universities began providing software to activate the initial rides on what we used to call the Information Highway. As the first image slowly rolled down the screen I felt a sudden surge of pleasure, entirely out of proportion to the banal content beginning to appear on the monitor. Balky at first, the software eventually worked and the first full color image lit up my screen. It was digital magic — positively sublime. With the arrival of graphical browsers, the Internet was opened to all of us, and Google, with help from early government investment in information technology, took off to become, behind Apple, the second richest corporation in the world.

By 1993 the Internet was so widespread that the *New Yorker* magazine could publish a cartoon that remains its most viewed. It features a dog sitting in front of a computer screen and telling a fellow canine, "On the Internet, nobody knows you're a dog." For much of the world, especially in developed countries, the Internet is nothing short of the dominant means of electronic communication. This makes it vitally important to understand how it is changing and what that means for the billions who rely on Internet communication every day. Even as Silicon Valley celebrated the Internet's adulthood, the Next Internet was emerging from infancy, hastening the arrival of what might reasonably be called the post-Internet world. Google acknowledged as much when in a revealing 2015 interview, the company's head of search declared that the search engine, which helped to define the original Internet, was now a "legacy" system (a euphemism for "still useful but soon destined for the trash heap"). Now Google, along with other large firms and small startups, is working on new forms of mobile-friendly search engines appropriate to the Next Internet.

THE WEB: DEEP AND DARK

The Internet is not the entirety of the digital world. In fact, it contains a fraction of what is located in what is called the Deep Web and the Dark Web. The Internet that most of us know is a vast store of data accessible through a web browser like Firefox, Safari, or Chrome and a search engine, most likely Google's, though some still look things up on Microsoft's Bing, or Verizon's Yahoo. The Deep Web contains databases that standard search engines are not able to reach but which require software provided by their managers. The Deep Web includes the private files of corporations, which permit, for example, employees of Apple to access the company's sales records and legal documents, and those of governments, such as the medical files of health care recipients and the locations of drone targets kept by the United States Cyber Command. Then there is the Dark Web, which is available to those who know how to use specialized software and need anonymity. Developed by the U.S. Navy, the Dark Web provides some cover for investigative journalists as well as for those needing to mask criminal activity. So in addition to helping reporters evade government scrutiny, it makes possible a marketplace for banned goods, including illegal drugs like opioids. Indeed, the Dark Web has been identified as a key instrument for fentanyl distribution in the United States. While this book will reference these less well-known corners of the digital world, most of it concentrates on those digital quadrants we visit the most, using tools like Google search, the Safari browser, and the software that makes possible one-click shopping with Amazon, Gmail or Apple's iCloud, and social media sites run by Facebook, Instagram, Snapchat, and Twitter.

There is also a web outside the formal orbit of the Internet that I would be remiss not to mention. The eminent

philosopher Willard Van Orman Quine advised us to consider the web inside our minds. We contain, he argued, a
"web of belief" that includes the ideas we cherish, which
occupy the center, and those connected to this core to form a
network of powerful ideological forces. Rather than hosting
a discrete collection of beliefs, our minds tie these together in
a more or less connected system that assesses new ideas and
beliefs in terms of how well they can fit into the "web of
belief." Well before cognitive psychology verified this view,
Quine understood the power and resilience of belief systems,
something especially important for those who scratch their
heads in disbelief over how supporters of Brexit and Donald
Trump remained enthusiastic in the face of so much evidence
challenging their views. We bring this web to all that we
encounter, including the webs of Internet social media that
are so influential today. There is no denying social media's
influence, but it is important to recognize that this influence is
tempered and often limited by our internal web of information and beliefs.

GRAND CONVERGENCES

This book is about how societies are becoming digital in a
post-Internet world. It focuses on the significance of major
transformations resulting from the convergence of Cloud
Computing, Big Data Analytics, and the Internet of Things,
the primary technological systems that make up the Next
Internet. Put simply, the Cloud stores and processes information in data centers; Big Data Analytics provides the tools
to analyze and make us of it; and the Internet of Things
connects sensor-equipped devices to electronic communication networks. Building on my 2014 book, *To the Cloud*,
I describe the essential elements of these three key

technological forces in the digital world and assess their social significance. Its central argument is that the Cloud, Big Data, and the Internet of Things comprise an increasingly integrated system that is accelerating the decline of a democratic, decentralized, and open-source Internet. There is nothing inevitable about this outcome. The Next Internet can be a tool to expand democracy, empower people worldwide, provide for more of life's necessities, and advance social equality. Instead, it is now primarily used to enlarge the commodification and militarization of the world. This trend is not inevitable, but concerted political and policy interventions are required to reverse it.

Understanding the digital world, and especially the transition to the Next Internet, requires more than explaining technologies. It also needs perspectives or ways to think about today's social upheavals. Specific details matter but so too do ways of seeing them. In addition to providing essential information on the Next Internet, I hope to improve on the capacity to understand today's communication technology by offering tools for reflection that, in the words of the great cultural theorist Raymond Williams, offer an "extra edge of consciousness" to understand the modern world. For this I primarily turn to *political economy*, which helps comprehend the power relations that shape the digital world, and *cultural studies*, which contributes to understanding how we make sense of it. The former leads us to carefully examine the power of today's technology leaders, primarily Apple, Google, Microsoft, Facebook, and Amazon, as well as governments whose intelligence agencies and armies depend on digital to project power. Cultural Studies explain how we make meaning in the world. Specifically, it explores how we invest technology with the desire for community, for emotional attachments, for guides to our place in the world, for a wisp of magic, and for a sense of the sublime that lifts us out of the banality of everyday life. Taken together, these converging ways of seeing digital technology provide more than a collection of facts about the post-Internet world, they offer powerful visions to understand it, and imagine solutions to its challenges.

A WEB OF PROBLEMS

We need these visions because the Next Internet will pose significant social problems including the concentrated power of a few global companies and the governments they work with, growing militarization, environmental devastation, the widespread commodification of personal information, unprecedented surveillance, and near universal automation. As a result, we need citizens who are not only familiar with these problems and can distinguish the old from the new Internet, the Cloud from the Internet of Things, and Google from Amazon. Our times require a keen sense of how to think critically, using the conceptual tools that political-economic and cultural approaches provide. Moreover, *Becoming Digital* recognizes that, even as the analog world remains important, there is no turning back from digital. Rather, we urgently need to advance citizen control over the core technologies, the data we generate, and how they are used. To that end, the book argues for making new use of an old concept, the public utility, which has historically been applied to the allocation of water, electricity, and other essential resources. The public utility concept has also appeared as a key focus of debate throughout the history of computing and, with the rise of centralized data storage and processing, made possible by Cloud Computing, it figures prominently in current debates about how to govern information resources.

THE ROAD AHEAD

Becoming Digital begins by describing how we arrived at today's Internet by focusing on the conflicting tendencies that marked its earliest days as a research communication network linking a handful of institutions. The combination of corporate and government funding, particularly by the Department of Defense, and loosely organized, collaborative projects bringing together university, corporate, and government research labs, delivered a complex mix. This included a tendency to hierarchy and regimentation, growing out of a Cold War mentality favoring centralized planning against what was perceived to be a unified Communist foe in possession of the most advanced technologies. But it also featured decentralized elements emerging from the experimental culture of the Internet's inventors, as well as the military objective that called for a fully distributed and robust network able to survive a major war, including a nuclear conflagration. Over the years, corporations realized the financial value of the Internet, especially the potential to deliver customized advertising to users whose every click could easily be monitored and recorded. In short order, the network grew to become a massively successful commercial instrument, even as it retained some of its original, decentralized, elements. The result is a global system of communication that is complex, contradictory, and contested by individual users, governments, businesses, and social movement organizations throughout the world.

Becoming Digital proceeds to describe how the fundamental structure and guiding values of the Internet are changing with the growth of Cloud Computing, Big Data Analytics, and the Internet of Things. It defines and describes the key characteristics of each with particular attention to how they are converging and becoming embedded in everyday life.

Cloud Computing is a system that provides data storage, software applications, and information technology services to fee-paying customers. These range from individuals who pay Amazon Web Services to store and process data that used to be kept on their laptop hard drive to the world's largest banks, which rely, for example, on Salesforce.com to manage their workforce and marketing divisions. Cloud Computing is transforming data storage, software and service delivery by shifting these functions from personal and corporate data centers to the Cloud.

Cloud data centers are more than giant warehouses that store data. They are closer to information factories that take data fed to their tens of thousands of servers by telecommunications cables and satellites and then process it to produce results that add value to the original data. Weather data becomes weather forecasts, medical data becomes a flu outbreak prediction, population data becomes a plan to build or close schools, crime data becomes police deployment, and so on. We increasingly hear references to Big Data or analytics to describe the application of statistical tools to very large data sets to develop predictive algorithms. For big data enthusiasts, these techniques eliminate the need for traditional approaches that rely on historical, theoretical, or qualitative understandings because what amounts to digital positivism enables the numbers to speak for themselves. The Cloud and Big Data are intimately connected to the singular reliance on quantitative analysis that allows companies to profit from packaging and selling enormous stores of data and also makes it possible for governments to extend their ability to monitor, manage, and control citizens. Moreover, when married to artificial intelligence systems, they can be used to determine whether we qualify for a mortgage, whether we are likely to commit a crime, and whether we qualify for an organ transplant.

The incentive to invest in the Cloud and Big Data expands exponentially with the Internet of Things, a system that embeds sensors and processors in everyday objects as well as in people. These are used to scan, monitor, record, and communicate online about the operation of things (Does my living room need more heat?) and the behavior of people (What is my blood pressure?). What the original Internet did for people, the Internet of Things does for objects and devices. No longer limited to building networks of human communication, the Internet of Things makes use of the Cloud and Big Data to create a global, centralized, and commodified system of communication among objects, as well as people. It promises to revolutionize industrial and informational practices, rationalize global supply chains, create so-called smart cities and homes, reconstitute offices and factories, and vastly expand the ability to monitor the body. Our Wi-Fi-enabled thermostats and step-counting smart phones represent the early days of Internet-based devices. However, given the commercial potential to measure and monitor everything and everybody, development is proceeding rapidly.

The convergence of Cloud Computing, Big Data Analytics, and the Internet of Things marks a new stage in digital development, a genuine ontological shift in the emerging post-Internet world. It not only deepens the tendency to experience others primarily through technological mediation. It also fundamentally shifts the relationship between humans and digital machines. The original Internet required an external device, such as a computer, tablet, or smart phone, to which one logged on to connect and communicate. Less an external means of communication, the Next Internet's digital networks are embedded everywhere, including inside us. They are enabling constant and ubiquitous connections to sensor-equipped objects, and to the scanners worn on, and placed in, our bodies. As with electricity, but far more powerfully, digital technology greatly expands its influence even as it withdraws into the woodwork of life. The human—computer divide is increasingly becoming an anachronism. For now, it means a steady integration of humans and machines. But it promises a future that raises fundamental questions for all of our institutions as we proceed to what some expect will be the trans-human world ahead.

Following a chapter on the technologies that comprise the immediate post-Internet world, *Becoming Digital* describes the significance of these developments with chapters on their political-economic and then on their bodily and cultural significance. I begin with political economy not to suggest any special privileging but simply as an appropriate starting point. Using the formal term, political economy is *mutually constituted* with culture at every level of their development. Both embody power and culture. The personal, the politicized body, is political, and the political, the body politic, is personal. I follow the chapter on technologies with one on political economy because it maps key corporate and government participants that reappear throughout the remainder of the book. These include the tech industry led by a handful of mainly U.S. companies that, on August 1, 2016, became the five most valuable corporations in the world. From first to fifth, they are Apple, Google, Microsoft, Amazon, and Facebook. Market caps change from time to time, but when assessing the power of Big Tech, it is important to acknowledge that it was the first time that five companies in the same industry led the list of the most valuable in the world. This was no fluke. On June 1, 2017, all five in their same respective positions, topped the market cap list. As if to add an exclamation point to this statement, on June 6, 2017 the annual list of the top 100 brands reported that these same companies led the way as the most valuable brands in the world. The only difference is that Google heads the brand list with Apple in second place.

The ability of these companies to dominate the digital world and fend off competitors has benefited enormously from close ties to the U.S. government, especially its military and intelligence agencies. Indeed, despite the occasional spat, there is an increasingly close connection between Silicon Valley and the military, which aims to apply the Valley's technologies to substantially expand remote warfare, especially through the global deployment of weaponized drones. With the decline of industry competitors from the United Kingdom and Europe, the United States faces only China for control over digital systems. Led by the giant Alibaba along with Baidu, Tencent, Huawei, and Wanda, and also with considerable government support, China is now a significant force in the emerging world of ubiquitous digital technology. The chapter concludes by situating the clash between the United States and China in the context of wider struggles about the global political economy, especially trade, culture, and military expansion.

Chapter four demonstrates that with the promise to transform and individuate the scanning and tracking of personal and interpersonal life, digital technologies are more than instruments in political-economic and geopolitical conflicts. They are also a force for control over individual bodies and social relationships. Indeed, the expectation of unprecedented commodification and control at the micro level, as Next Internet technologies are inserted into everyday life, fuels much of the feverish competition at the macro level. The chapter begins by addressing the creation of a quantified and commodified self through the development and promotion of sensor-equipped products that track the performance of bodily organs and their functions, gather and store data in the Cloud, and apply analytics to draw conclusions, develop algorithms, and make predictions. Interest in measuring and monitoring all aspects of human functioning extends beyond the tech companies that design and manufacture devices. Advertisers are tapping into the vast market potential; insurers are eager to sharpen their predictive models; employers are using these devices to closely monitor workers; and governments deploy them to better manage and control citizens.

Such major leaps in technical capacity are accompanied by supporting cultural myths, understood not as false visions of reality, but as stories we tell each other to help us cope with the inexplicable, with accelerating change, and, ultimately, with the knowledge of our own mortality. It has been said that we make myths whenever we make technologies and the transition to the Next Internet is no exception. The new digital world is supported by two prominent stories, including first the *singularity* or the promise of fully integrating human bodies and machines. Believers expect that the resulting meta-humans will vastly expand productive capabilities, overcome the conflicts that have historically divided people and societies, and perhaps even achieve immortality. The chapter also takes up a primary myth propelling the Internet of Things, the centuries-old promise of bringing *things* to life. Today's conjurers embed intelligence in everyday devices and, whether or not we call it "artificial," this imagined power feeds utopian visions that ease the fears of radical technological change.

Chapter five addresses emerging problems, including the vulnerabilities unleashed by reliance on a digital world primarily led by a handful of private corporations and driven by commercialization. Problems also include expansion in militarization as weaponized drones and robotic warriors take to the battlefield. Additionally it takes up the serious issue of environmental degradation from the massive growth in the power requirements for Next Internet systems and in electronic or e-waste produced by discarded hardware; surveillance by corporations, governments, and hackers; and, finally, the challenge of a transformed global division of labor which, along with automation and artificial intelligence, threatens workers and their jobs.

The final chapter considers the prospects for solving these problems. There is no guarantee that the convergence of the Cloud, Big Data, and the Internet of Things will meet the goals of its corporate and government supporters. The Internet of Things in particular has proven to be highly vulnerable to hackers and data thieves who have already used Wi-Fi-enabled devices to attack and take down networks. The difficult task of securing networks may lead to market failures for many promising applications. Indeed, some look at the growing popularity of music on vinyl (now surpassing in value digital downloads), print books, and in-person meetups, particularly among young people, as signs of a tilt back to analog. We may very well be increasingly digital, but analog communication is far from consigned to the dustbin of history.

Chapter six also examines the work of those who believe another world, including another Internet, is possible by pressing for greater citizen control over communication and information resources. It considers the importance of structural and transactional social movements that are fighting to address major problems, including struggles to oppose concentrated corporate control over the digital world; opposition to militarism; the creation of environmentally sustainable information systems; resistance to the growth of a surveillance society by fighting for the human right to, and the human necessity of, privacy; and the global movement for a guaranteed living income. Increasing interest is focusing on the public utility model that provided the foundation for widespread access to essential resources like water and power. The utility model also has deep roots in the history of computing. Although the recent growth of massive, centralized data systems expands corporate and government control over information, it is also creating conditions that support genuine citizen control. The convergence of Cloud Computing, Big Data Analytics, and the Internet of Things is often described as laying the groundwork for a utility model of communication. It increasingly resembles a utility in all but ownership and control. These remain primarily in the hands of private corporations that act like monopolies that dominate producer markets and monopsonies that control purchaser markets. Establishing public control over these markets would not only expand public access to the rich resource of the Next Internet. It would also better enable citizens to address problems arising from the new digital world. Specifically, more people would have the opportunity to make socially beneficial uses of the information now routinely given up to private corporations and governments with no compensation. *Becoming Digital* concludes with a discussion of how an electronic communication system based on the public information utility model could help realize the powerful democratic visions that inspired so much of the original Internet.

CHAPTER 2

CONVERGING TECHNOLOGIES

Technology is the active human interface with the material world.

— Ursula K. Le Guin

TECHNOLOGY AND SOCIETY

By starting with a chapter on technologies, I do not mean to imply anything about causality in the relationship of machines to society. There are those who, in the interest of explanation or simply as a shortcut, argue for technological determinism. The plow gave us feudalism; the steam engine brought a manufacturing society; the computer, an information age. Others go to the opposite extreme and believe that technologies are determined or shaped by society. In essence, machines are no more than congealed social relationships. Take apart a plow, a steam engine or a computer, they say, and we are left with the dominant social forms that existed at their creation. Accordingly, emerging feudal, industrial, and informational societies create the technologies appropriate to the social relations and structures of power of the time. Both of these views are useful but I believe that it is more useful to take a position somewhere in between the two. Formally put, technologies, societies, and individuals mutually constitute one another. To put it less formally, they contribute to each others' creation and development at every stage, setting important limits without any essential causal determination.

TO THE CLOUD

I begin with technologies because readers will be less familiar with the major elements that make up the Next Internet and because technological convergence represents a fundamental change from the network most people have used for the last three decades. Cloud Computing preceded data analytics and the Internet of Things and got its name from the network diagrams that engineers used to describe a network. Typically, network nodes were drawn to look like clouds. As anyone who has visited a massive, server-filled, windowless data center can attest, there is nothing cloud-like about its look and feel. In its present form, the Cloud has been available to individual and institutional users for slightly over a decade. One reason why some see today's Cloud as little more than a marketing ploy is because a form of what we now call Cloud Computing was prominent in the early years of computerization. Then it was referred to as time-sharing to identify the practice of computing on terminals linked to a central computer where the data and intelligence were stored. As a graduate student, I fed punch cards into a mainframe input device in order to have my research processed and analyzed. There were no personal computers back in the 1960s and early 1970s. We were all tethered to what today would be called a data center, albeit considerably more primitive than the vast information factories that fill acres of land today.

This began to end in 1975 when the first personal computers appeared and people slowly adapted to devices that stored programs and data on their own computers and disks. In this respect and on a far grander scale, Cloud Computing takes us back to the future, where the electronic tether now connects us to data centers. Cloud Computing does repackage an old idea but one might also say that the package looks so very different today that, marketing claims aside, it does merit a new identity. This was signaled in a *New Yorker* magazine cartoon that, like the one announcing the arrival of the Internet, lifted the curtain on Cloud Computing in popular discourse. It featured a young boy looking sheepishly at his teacher who expects him to deliver an assignment. Instead, he delivers a new riff on an old excuse: "The Cloud ate my homework." Cloud Computing had arrived.

The Cloud is one of the few information technologies that actually comes with an official definition. Shortly after the marketing departments of Cloud companies began to spread publicity and pump up the hype, U.S. government technology officials ordered agencies to adopt Cloud Computing. Puzzled, many responded with, "What's Cloud Computing?" As a result, the government agency responsible for expertise in science and technology was asked to produce a definition and came up with this: "Cloud computing is a model for enabling convenient, on-demand network access to a shared pool of configurable computing resources (e.g., networks, servers, storage, applications, and services) that can be rapidly provisioned and released with minimal management effort or service provider interaction."[1] I cannot say with certainty that this completely satisfied the demand for clarity. Other analysts offered more pointed definitions, including "computing on someone else's computer," "the next step in outsourcing IT jobs," and "a bullsh*t marketing term," a definition

I actually heard given by an IT expert at a cloud computing promotional event.

Each of these definitions is accurate. Cloud computing is a system that moves data stored on individual computers and in the IT departments of institutions to large, distant data centers operated by companies that charge for storage and use. Amazon is the largest of such firms. For over a decade its Amazon Web Services division has benefited from the ability to continuously drop prices through cross-subsidies from its many other divisions, to take market share (now at about one-third of the cloud market) and build a global network of data centers. In addition to warehousing data for a fee, cloud providers offer software and applications that enable users to carry out operations without having to store and update software on their own machines. In addition to offering storage, Google, for example, provides its Gmail service through the Cloud. Similarly, Microsoft, which is second largest in cloud storage, now delivers its popular writing, spreadsheet, and other productivity software through the Cloud on a monthly subscription basis. Apple provides data storage through its iCloud along with such additions as device syncing and enhancements for those who store their mail, music, and video files in the Cloud. To round out the familiar examples, Facebook has created a virtual community in the Cloud for its two billion users. Mastery of the Cloud is one of the primary reasons why Amazon, Google, Microsoft, Apple, and Facebook are the most valuable companies in the world. Some cloud businesses also offer services that make it possible for companies to outsource some or all of their sales, personnel, accounting, legal, and other functions. The company Salesforce.com is a prime example of a cloud-based business that draws from its network of data centers to manage marketing and human relations for firms of every size.

For the convenience of offloading data, software and services, individual and institutional users pay a regular subscription fee that can also vary with usage. This has proven incentive enough to create a global construction boom in data centers as large firms and some specialized medium-sized companies jockey for a share of the growing market. In addition to subscriber fees, companies have access to vast stores of valuable data, particularly when it can be grist for the big data mill. For example, Google and Facebook use the information that flows through their data centers on the email and social media posts of users to sell customized advertising. Moreover, data is used to develop algorithms that businesses and governments are willing to pay for because it helps them to predict the activities of markets and people. On the other side, individual users benefit by lessening the need to store data and software on their own computers. As the digital world has become less safe for users, many would rather put their trust in established commercial providers to protect their data, or at least use more secure systems for backup, than to rely solely on their own devices. The same holds, only on a much larger scale, for businesses and other large institutional users. These benefit by reducing the need to expand their own IT facilities. Who needs an onsite data or server center when another company will provide storage for your company or government agency? Why bother buying new software that your IT staff has to regularly update and debug when a cloud company like Microsoft will provide the latest versions online? More radically, why employ a large IT staff, as well as accountants, sales, personnel, legal, and other costly staff professionals when a cloud company like Salesforce will do the work for you? Cloud Computing begins to make financial sense when it can be used to cut professional staff and outsource to the Cloud.

Seeing opportunities to cut staff also inspired governments to hop onto the cloud bandwagon early and to spend lavishly. Facing budget cuts, many domestic agencies turned to the Cloud to save on IT costs. Intelligence and defense agencies, with far fewer budget worries, saw the Cloud as an opportunity to centralize operations for increased security and control. The National Security Agency, which became famous, or infamous, because of whistle blower Edward Snowden's revelations about the extent of its legal and illegal spy operations, has built one of the world's largest Cloud facilities in a secure Utah location. The Central Intelligence Agency also moved quickly to construct its own facilities and it also gave a contract to Amazon to purchase $600 million worth of cloud services. It is not unusual for government agencies, including those operating in a highly sensitive environment, to outsource at least some of its cloud requirements in order to build redundancy into its systems and create strong ties to key private sector organizations. The ability to call on its commercial friends comes in handy when the CIA faces intensely embarrassing situations, like the Wikileaks revelation that it routinely hacks ordinary consumer devices like Samsung's "smart" televisions, recording the conversations of households even when the sets are turned off, and analyzing them in the CIA Cloud.

These significant incentives are offset by technical challenges. No minor investment, data centers are big projects that require careful planning if the interconnected system comprising tens of thousands of servers, switching equipment, and telecommunications facilities linking the facility to the world are to function properly. In addition to requiring real estate, cloud data centers need massive energy supplies to power servers and to keep them sufficiently cool to avoid overheating. Most people in the business are aware of the overheating incident in which, were it not for a nearby shop that sold electrical fans to panicked employees, Facebook's first server center might have completely overheated and taken down the company. Finding low cost energy deals is not easy nor is locating inexpensive supplies of the water essential to keep servers cool. As a result, cloud facilities are often located in cold climates with abundant energy and water supplies, a reason why Canada's province of Quebec, which has both, and especially Montreal, with its burgeoning tech industry, has become a location of choice for big companies such as Google and Amazon. On the down side, however, remote locations often mean high telecommunications costs to connect data centers to the global grid. Furthermore, given the sensitivity of both servers and data, cloud facilities cannot be located in places where earthquakes and weather disasters would spell catastrophe. In addition, customers demanding quality 24/7 service do not tolerate downtime. The only solution is the installation of expensive backup systems that can take over when the electricity grid goes down. While a great deal of understandable concern, thought, and investment goes into the need for security against hackers and intruders, climate change may prove to be an equally formidable challenge.

Users face significant challenges as well. Parting with data to save on storage costs might make economic sense, but it also means giving up the feeling of control that proximity often provides. Can you really trust a cloud provider to care for your data as much as you do? What happens to your data if a provider goes out of business or just decides to focus on something else, the next big thing that suddenly looks like a lucrative opportunity? It is in the interest of cloud providers to lock in customers with long-term contracts that contain expensive additions. What sounds good today often proves excessively costly tomorrow. Moreover, customers have to trust their providers to offer sufficient security. While they have many incentives to maintain a clean Cloud, those offering cloud services have to make delicate judgments that balance this requirement against the growing costs of adequate security.

It is also advantageous for providers to build data centers in numerous locations around the world because doing so creates new markets, advances global connectivity, and diminishes dependence on specific markets. But it also means subjecting data to different legal jurisdictions. For years, authorities in the United States sought access to files stored in a Microsoft data center located in Ireland which U.S. law-enforcement authorities maintained was central to a major criminal investigation. Microsoft and the government of Ireland resisted U.S government demands, citing EU jurisdiction and regulations protecting the data. The U.S. government lost that case but filed another one, this time against Google, to obtain emails stored on foreign servers. Apple, Amazon, Microsoft, and Cisco filed briefs to support Google and the outcome is uncertain. What is certain is that, as the Cloud becomes an essential feature of the Next Internet, situations like these will become more pervasive. Canadians worry about their data stored on U.S. servers, which subjects data to the Patriot Act and other legislation that justifies widespread surveillance of information practices. What will they and others think when their data is stored on servers in China or Russia?

The cloud computing industry has dealt with these issues in numerous ways. From the start it created tiers of services and levels of control that have provided some customization for users who demanded it. It also distinguished those who use and trust cloud services only for data storage from those who want, and trust the cloud company to provide a platform for functions like email (Gmail), and office software (Microsoft). Customers not keen to rely on Google for email can download their own software and store their emails on their own computers or in IT department servers. Again, this is no simple matter. Google might take some of the work out of email and for a price that only amounts to having ads appear alongside mail. But it also means storing mail in data centers whose location, and hence legal jurisdiction, is not clear. In addition, some cloud providers serve as robust alternatives to in-house functions replacing all or part of entire departments by offering traditional business services. Whether it is Salesforce.com or Uptime Legal Systems, this form of Cloud Computing, referred to as Software as a Service (SaaS), means giving up the greatest amount of control and requires the most trust. It is one thing to store your data on someone else's computer, quite another to outsource core functions like sales, legal, and personnel to another firm.

Alongside these service levels, cloud providers distinguish between public and private services. The Public Cloud is for those with the least need or concern for security and privacy. Although cloud companies insist that they provide the highest level of data protection and secure services for everyone, storing data in the Public Cloud is like bringing it to a warehouse that is also used by tens of thousands of other customers. A public cloud data center takes on all customers and attracts them with the lowest rates in the industry. Amazon pioneered the Public Cloud and by taking advantage of economies of scale continues to lead the sector. Those who want and can pay for more security turn to the Private Cloud. These are the equivalent of gated communities in the Cloud where security is tighter and servers are sequestered for higher paying customers. The distinction between public and private Clouds varies by company and there are different grades of service within each. Industry associations help develop standards with the financial services sector understandably taking a lead. As a result, standards have been adopted for "bank-grade" Cloud systems, more secure than those typically found in a private cloud service. There are also various hybrid cloud systems that bring together features of both public and private clouds for those who want more security but cannot afford a fully private cloud provider. These often also include some data storage and processing on the customer's premises and access to some company data in the event of an outage or a hacking attack on one or more of the cloud provider's facilities.

Before leaving this discussion of public and private cloud services, it is important to consider just what the term "public" means here, if only to specify what adding an "extra edge of consciousness" actually means. Unlike the way it is used in discussions of public space, citizenship, and democracy, the public in Public Cloud refers to a customer's choice to buy services from a commercial provider, typically through a subscription or usage fee but also by accepting advertising. This is a far cry from the traditional view of a public as a set of citizens whose right to participate in a democratic society requires the equitable distribution of the tools for them to do so. A genuine Public Cloud would set aside access to secure cloud services as a fundamental right and a requirement for democracy. In this respect there is no Public Cloud. There are varieties of private Cloud Computing that come with a range of price tags and security levels. The erosion of the concept of the public has important consequences, particularly as societies move into the next phase of the Internet. If planning for the future of one of democracy's central tools is burdened with historical amnesia over a central principle, it becomes even more difficult to consider the future information space as anything other than private, commercial, and commodified.

Recent years have brought into the mix what is called Edge Computing, a new form of outsourced data processing so named because it pushes processing and intelligence out from the data center to the edges of networks. It warrants close scrutiny because it may challenge the dominance of Cloud Computing. Edge Computing emerged from a debate about whether cloud data centers are capable of managing the complex requirements of new devices that require near instantaneous data analysis and tight security. The automated car, what has been described as a data center on wheels, drones, industrial robots, embedded medical devices, all of these test the capacity of large, centralized data centers to operate with efficiency and timeliness. As a result, companies are exploring the potential to embed some of the intelligence contained in the traditional cloud inside the devices themselves, thereby speeding up automated decision-making (e.g., sensors warning of a lane-hopping car up ahead) and permitting customized security. This would depart from, for example, how smart phones operate. When I go out for a walk and my data craving self (more about that in chapter four) checks to see if I have made my daily goal of 15,000 steps, I receive the results from a communication between my phone and a cloud data center which stores my iPhone information in the iCloud. Edge Computing contains the Cloud in the device.

Some believe that Edge Computing will replace the Cloud by reopening the potential for distributed networks of millions, if not billions, of devices. Others foresee a division of labor with the distant cloud data center providing strategic decision-making, for example, advising and carrying out software and firmware updates, and leaving detailed operational decision-making to the edge-equipped device. Over the past 40 years I have observed hundreds of forecasts announcing the Next Big Thing that will rock the industry and society. Back in the 1960s, for example, color televisions were expected to soon give way to 3D. In the 1970s videophones were just around the corner. In the 1980s it was the interactive device called videotex. Few make it beyond the dream lists of prognosticators because the existing dominant technology adapts and absorbs the challenger, because the new device or system arrives too soon, or because the problems it solves are not worth the investment. Nevertheless, Edge Computing bears watching if only to remind us that cloud data centers may not be up to the task of automation's next wave. Such an outcome would have significant impacts on America's dominant tech firms because they all have invested heavily in the Cloud.

Cloud Computing has been able to fend off challenges partly because it has been marketed extraordinarily well. After all, the principle of Cloud Computing is not at all new and there is nothing especially stunning about how it works. Moreover, as chapter five addresses, there are numerous social problems associated with the role of Cloud Computing in the Next Internet. Effective marketing was absolutely essential to sell the necessity of filling the world with giant data factories and convincing individuals and institutions to move to the Cloud. Beginning with the image of the ethereal, if not quite immaterial, puffy white cloud, that replaced the big, ugly data center in the minds of potential users, Cloud Computing benefitted from a global advertising campaign, including early, very expensive ads telecast during the U.S. Super Bowl, annually the highest rated broadcast in America. Nearly all of the major cloud companies produced ads but the prize for *chutzpah* went to Microsoft for a widely circulated video. It featured a mom about to take a photograph of her family. Like most families it was hard to get everyone to sit still, smile and appear, well, family-like and the photos reflected this. Undaunted, mom turns "to the Cloud" where she finds photos featuring faces of her family members in smiling repose and swaps them for the desultory images she has just taken. The result, "finally a photo I can share without ridicule." Then the *coup de grâce*, "Windows gives me the family nature never could."

Along with the big ad campaigns, Cloud Computing benefited from free publicity compliments of promotional blogs and posts by self-proclaimed industry experts who vouched for the revolutionary significance of the Cloud. Complementing these forms of advertising and pseudo-advertising, leading private think tanks, including Gartner, McKinsey, Deloitte, and Forrester, produced reports concluding the same thing, only in more scientific language. Even the World Economic Forum, the leading intellectual force behind neoliberal globalization, chimed in with its own report calling on the world to join the cloud revolution. Inevitably these reports would find their way onto blog posts to produce a supportive echo chamber. Finally, the cloud's arrival was fortuitously timed because it appeared just when Silicon Valley was waking up to the need to build its lobbying presence in Washington on a number of issues ranging from immigration to surveillance. As a result, proponents of Cloud Computing were able to create a strong promotional force just when legislators were learning about some of the social and environmental problems associated with the Internet.

All of this benefitted the cloud computing industry and especially the major U.S. participants. These were also fortunate enough to emerge at a time when Europe's telecommunications providers, including Siemens, Ericsson, Nokia and Canada's Nortel, and Blackberry, which once dominated the industry, fell into decline. Failing to foresee and take advantage of the burgeoning Internet and unable to keep up with Apple's near universally popular iPhone, these companies survived, some barely, as much lesser participants in a global information technology upheaval. That left Amazon, Google, Microsoft, Apple, Facebook, IBM, Salesforce.com,

Rackspace, and a few others to control the market. The only genuine challenge to U.S. domination in the Cloud comes from China where the giant firm Alibaba is using its power in China's domestic cloud marketplace to build an international cloud business sufficient to take on the major U.S. firms. The next chapter addresses the political ramifications of this development. Now it is time to turn to Big Data Analytics, the second leg of the Next Internet, in its own right a major force in the success of Cloud Computing.

THE NUMBERS WILL SPEAK FOR THEMSELVES

Converging with Cloud Computing, Big Data Analytics refers to a system for the quantitative analysis of large data sets. In spite of the proliferation of fancy new titles that fuel enthusiasm, like data science professional, there is very little that a social scientist would find novel in the big data approach. It generally involves taking a large, often massive, and, almost always, quantitative batch of data, and examining the specific ways the data do or do not cohere or correlate. The aim is to draw conclusions about current behavior and attitudes and go on to make predictions. Specifically, big data analysts produce algorithms or a set of rules that specify conclusions to be drawn or actions to be taken under specific conditions. Facebook, for example, takes the data generated by its two billion or so users and relates the "likes" associated with posts about everything from celebrities, companies, and politicians to views about society, products, and, of course, cats. These enable the company to develop profiles on its subscribers, which Facebook sells to marketers who target users with customized ads sent to their Facebook pages. Google does the same for search topics and, until public pressure forced Google to announce that it would end the practice by the end of 2017, the company has scanned the content of Gmail. Amazon creates profiles of its users based on searches and purchases on its site.

What fuels the enthusiasm for Big Data is the massive growth in the amount of information readily available for analysis because it is now organized in an accessible form in cloud data centers. The term "data mining" is appropriate because it suggests that the payoff is in finding valuable nuggets in the relationships among seemingly unconnected behavior and attitudes, what is referred to as "productivising data." The early development of the Cloud and Big Data, particularly the massive information gathered by search engines, powered predictions of an intellectual revolution that would sweep away traditional academic disciplines and research approaches. Leading the charge was Chris Anderson who in 2008 wrote in *Wired* magazine about "The End of Theory." With enough data and applied mathematics we can finally declare: "Out with every theory of human behaviour, from linguistics to sociology. Forget taxonomy, ontology, and psychology. Who knows why people do what they do? The point is they do it, and we can track and measure it with unprecedented fidelity. With enough data, the numbers speak for themselves."[2] Anderson was not alone, as devotees from the sciences to sociology and even the humanities repeated this rallying cry, if with slightly toned down language. The prospect of taking the banality of everyday existence and turning it into a digital sublime of predictive power sparked talk of revolutionizing our ways of knowing and of creating new ways of being and doing.

Big Data promised to radically renew the philosophy of positivism that the nineteenth century social scientist August Comte took from the hard sciences and applied to understanding society. For Comte, empirical observations and the data of experience alone qualified for a true scientific understanding of the world. There would be no room for theory or what was called, disparagingly, metaphysical speculation. Today's versions of Comte aim for a *digital positivism* that realizes the French sociologist's goal of making the facts of life speak for themselves. To carry out this goal, corporations, government agencies, scholars, civil society organizations, and social movements dig into the data to find connections and create predictive algorithms. A new occupation, the data scientist, was created to lead the effort and universities developed new degree programs to train big data professionals.

The results were mixed and the messianic zeal for Big Data has somewhat abated. In 2012, the leading research company Gartner predicted that by 2020 there would be a shortage of 200,000 data scientists. Five years later it forecast that by 2020 automation would kill 40 percent of existing data scientist jobs. Nevertheless, along with the growth in data sets, analytics research is expanding across a wide range of applications. The largest beneficiaries are the big data collectors, including Google, primarily through its search engine and email program, Facebook, the overwhelming leader in social media, and Amazon, which gathers data on its retail customers to be stored and analyzed in its own cloud division Amazon Web Services. In addition to using this data internally to match user profiles to what customers like and purchase, Amazon sells the data to advertisers who market products and services on their own sites and on those target customers are likely to visit. So when I searched Google to learn whether the Nordstrom Rack store that just opened in my neighborhood had the running shoes I like, ads for the store began popping up on my New York Times site and on most others I searched. That is because research determined that it was worthwhile for the wholesale advertising purchaser to make this information available on other sites that share an interest in my profile. Completing the circle, retailers contract with companies that have access to my actual purchases through credit card data and other sources. In that way, they can determine what advertising actually leads to a buy and construct an algorithm that applies to people with my profile in order to predict the advertising that is likely to work in the future. Retailers also use Big Data to speed up price changes and determine product placement.

Although advertising and retail help drive big data research, there are many other applications. Amazon itself sells access to the data that manufacturers use to improve the time it takes to get products to market, to improve supply planning, and to forecast product demand. Utilities compare customer profiles with data collected from intelligent home and business meters to improve forecasting of energy needs and respond more effectively to changes in demand. From the drones that carry out aerial photography to precision monitoring of crop yields, water, and pesticide use, farmers are able to use data analytics to practice what is increasingly called "precision agriculture." Researchers in the health care industry make extensive use of Big Data to forecast the spread of communicable disease and develop algorithms to predict with precision rates of well-being and mortality among different populations. These results are understandably of great interest to risk assessors like insurance companies and credit bureaus, which use their own data to determine qualifications and set rates. With Big Data, risk assessment has become big business.

Governments have been making extensive use of Big Data at all levels. As the Edward Snowden revelations of 2013 and the WikiLeaks data dump of 2017 demonstrate, U.S. intelligence agencies have employed Big Data Analytics gathered in their own as well as in commercial cloud systems. Building profiles and carrying out sophisticated network analysis of potential terrorists, spy agencies provide the models for security and policing in the United States and wherever it has influence around the world. Moreover, law enforcement increasingly, and not without controversy, makes use of predictive analytics to forecast the neighborhoods and people who are likely to commit crimes.

Outside these areas, Big Data Analytics is an essential tool to deliver government services, determine eligibility and track users. Educational institutions have deployed analytics for some time, particularly to manage enrolments and, at the university level, to reach out to potential applicants and donors. As one would expect, scholars in the hard sciences make heavy use of big data tools, everything from high-energy particle research to a project that organizes the 25,240 notebook entries that Charles Darwin produced leading up to his *Origin of Species*. They are also increasingly deployed in the social sciences and even in the humanities. In fact, as a result of major U.S. government support, what is called the Digital Humanities movement incorporates Big Data to carry out with relative ease what were once daunting, if not impossible, quantitative research on the contents of written texts. While one might question the necessity of some of this research, for example, we now know that James Joyce leads major novelists in the use of exclamation points with 1,105 per 100,000 words, there is no doubt that the Digital Humanities has changed how scholars carry out research in centuries-old fields.

Given the inexorable growth of urbanization worldwide, big data researchers have made "smart cities" a special focus of attention with high hopes of using the data gathered on transportation, energy use, environmental pollution, waste management, and the health of citizens to create more liveable and sustainable urban areas. Cities like Oslo, Norway, Portland,

Oregon, and the Madrid suburb of Rivas Vaciamadrid, home to the Ecopolis smart city project, are notable examples.

Notwithstanding these growing applications, Big Data Analytics has not lived up to Anderson's forecast that it would radically transform research and bring about the end of theory. One reason why it has not sustained early expectations for revolutionizing applied social science, policy formation, and academic disciplines, is a series of highly criticized studies that demonstrated Big Data's limitations. In 2009, Google researchers published a study examining search terms associated with the percentage of visits to physicians where influenza-like symptoms were diagnosed. This enabled, they claimed, the prediction of flu outbreaks with almost no time lag (one day) as compared to the best that the U.S. Centers for Disease Control could provide (two weeks). If verified, this might qualify as the kind of radical research finding that inspired Chris Anderson's vision of sweeping away our intellectual past and replacing it all with numbers that speak for themselves. Optimism rose after the initial success, but the researchers' algorithm failed miserably in the 2012−2013 flu season when the model forecast higher than average levels of flu that did not materialize. It turned out that people were searching a lot more for flu information because they were more aware of the damage flu can do and because media saturation spread a panic over flu that sent people to their search engines in record numbers. Google promised to improve its model. But the damage was done. Often described as a tool to find a needle in a haystack, Google's researchers demonstrated that the needle could easily be lost again.

The Google flu fiasco gave way to stories about ethically challenged big data research at Facebook and the matchmaking dating service OKCupid. Facebook decided to engage in a big data-sized mass experiment to determine whether it was possible to use social media to influence emotional states. It did so by choosing 689,003 users whose news feeds were manipulated without their knowledge to present almost exclusively positive or negative stories. Using the standard obscure consent agreement that most people never read to justify the ethics of the project, Facebook was heavily criticized and Big Data got a big black eye. Following the furore that erupted over this 2014 story, OkCupid admitted that it too was engaging in user manipulation. The dating service was carrying out research to determine if love would blossom even if it recommended partners that its own algorithms had already determined were simply not compatible. The company was not helped by its justification: everybody does it. Big Data took another big hit.

Then there was the doctoral student who undermined one of the research pillars of the neoliberal globalization strategy, which policy-makers at the International Monetary Fund, the European Union and other powerful institutions had been using to promote austerity measures. The study in question was a big data analysis of the relationship between national debt and economic growth. Specifically it drew from massive historical data sets to justify the claim that once a nation's debt reaches 90 percent of its Gross Domestic Product, growth slows. The research was used to buttress painful economic measures, including cutbacks in government spending on social programs. These were justified as the necessary short-term pain that would lead to long-term social benefits. The authors became academic stars. All that ended when the student discovered major flaws in the research that significantly challenged the results. Many of the errors proved obvious, including spreadsheet mistakes, but others involved intense scrutiny of how variables were weighted. Such scrutiny is not easy in research involving large amounts of information and, while controversy continues to brew over the story, Big Data's big promises were once again under-mined. Many concluded that Big Data can easily lead to big errors that are hard to track but which carry big human consequences.

As if the world needed another example of Big Data's lim-itations, along came the election of President Donald J. Trump. Big Data was used throughout the two-year election cycle and then roundly criticized in the aftermath of the elec-tion. Building models based on historical polling of state and national races, almost all pollsters forecast a Clinton victory with a probability of anywhere from 70 to 99 percent with one major pollster agreeing, if Trump won, to eat a bug on live TV (he did). The reasons given for this failure seem end-less and some understandably defend Big Data because the popular vote margin predictions were generally upheld and because, in a story given very little attention, the Trump cam-paign successfully made use of analytics to slice and dice the American electorate to win just enough states to put him over the top. But there is no backing off from the conclusion that faith in Big Data played a significant role in the belief that Hilary Clinton would win, with relative ease, an Electoral College victory. There is also evidence that this faith may have influenced her campaign strategy. After all, advised by her analytics people that the important state of Wisconsin was a shoo-in, Ms. Clinton did not visit in the last six months of the campaign. Similar advice convinced her that Michigan was a lock and that Republican states like Arizona were in play. We do not know for sure but faith in big data-based forecasts may have caused some of her supporters to stay home from the polls. This is not an excuse for the campaign's other failures and there is no gainsaying the ultimate bril-liance of the Trump campaign's strategy. Like the Brexit campaign, it tapped into and exploited anger about the status quo that could not be easily measured by statistical techniques. Both events were major shocks and once again provided evidence that something is wrong with Big Data that needs to be fixed to avoid future failures that would threaten the legitimacy of the approach.

This may be the case. But having carried out research on both large and small data sets, I cannot conclude that there is anything inherently wrong in Big Data Analytics, assuming that it is carried out carefully and also provided that the methodology is viewed, and used, as one among several research approaches. Contrary to the dreams of enthusiasts, Big Data Analytics is not the answer to every question. It is especially not useful to apply Big Data to solve problems that may not actually exist or are less than significant. The tendency to address topics not because of their importance as social problems but rather because they can be easily quantified using one or another technological tool, what Evgeny Morozov aptly calls "solutionism," wastes resources, ignores genuinely significant issues, and does little for the reputation of scholarly research.

Big Data analysis requires a degree of care that is not sufficiently recognized. As the research on national debt and economic growth demonstrated, small errors like a few inaccurate spreadsheet cells, can have major negative consequences. Errors buried under a mountain of data can easily be left uncorrected and lead to inaccurate results. Moreover, even mountains of quantitative data are often no substitute for qualitative research whose findings result from in-depth interviews and actual observations of human behavior that reveal the fullness of human subjectivity. It is not easy, if at all possible, to understand how people make meaning out of their lives and their social situations with quantitative data alone. Quantitative research often tries to do so by assigning numerical values to subjective states. However, these are, at best, rough approximations that suggest more than they can actually warrant. Assigning a numerical value to "agree" and another to "strongly agree" might help create a large database, but actually say little about the qualitative feelings of respondents. Even if it were ethical for Facebook to carry out research on emotional states by manipulating newsfeeds, which most now agree it was not, one should doubt that its researchers could really determine the change in emotional states simply by assigning quantitative values to positive and negative user comments. This would at best be a very rough approximation, a precursor to methods, such as in-depth interviews, that are much more reliable for understanding changes in subjective states.

It is tempting and more than a little exciting to think that Big Data Analytics can sweep aside traditional approaches. But those who refuse to see it as just one among a set of approaches also miss the importance of theory and of historical context. Avoiding what have been the twin pillars of social research makes it easier to find causality in the correlations that big data analysts discover. But correlations are merely associations between variables, suggesting at best the strength of a relationship between, for example, search terms and the incidence of flu. Before Big Data euphoria promised an intellectual revolution, elementary social science explained that correlation is not causality. It still isn't. Apparent correlations are often spurious and therefore misleading because they can neglect another factor, like media attention to flu, that might lead people to increase their search for flu answers without any apparent symptoms.

A rich understanding of theory and context is the best way to avoid the problem of misinterpreting the results of correlational analysis. Theory provides the narrative that helps make sense from a mass of data. Best when it is carefully grounded in both data and past research, theory requires an appreciation of causality. Not necessarily the search for the sole determining force, causality can also mean setting limits and describing a process of mutual constitution. Data do not speak for themselves. We give data voice with theory.

Because Big Data tends to examine human behavior as a set of data points comprising discrete, individual events, it tends to resist the need to examine context and history. This is fundamentally misguided because behavior is not made up of distinct events and people are not data points. What we do, our behavior, and who we are, our character, are all deeply embedded in richly connected sequences. The popularity of stories is evidence that we understand this. The digital positivism of Big Data tends to neglect, if not reject, this view, seeing in our attraction to stories little more than evidence of a more primitive state that needs to be replaced by examining statistical relationships among a mass of discrete data points. To use the language of big data enthusiasts, unless used carefully, the approach that claims to find needles in haystacks often produces only bigger haystacks. Understanding haystack formation is the job of history, which makes it an important tool, one certainly not to be discarded in the race to embrace the new.

To summarize, Big Data would be far better an instrument for understanding the world if researchers, especially data scientists, paid explicit attention to the lived, qualitative experience of subjects over simply focusing on what can be represented in data. Big Data Analytics would be a far better approach if it paid attention to constructing causal arguments, rather than assuming that correlation is causation, which it clearly is not. Nor is causation a hammer with which to beat reality into submission. Causality sets limits, suggests relationships, and maps the processes of mutual constitution and multiple determination. In addition, Big Data would benefit from more attention to theory and not burden data with the need to explain itself. Finally, it would be a sharper tool if it rebalanced the tendency to unabashed *presentism* with a willingness to entertain the importance of history and context.

Problems aside, there remains significant support for Big Data. Some of this inevitably comes from the power of the method as a revenue-generating machine, particularly among the leaders of Big Tech such as Facebook and Google who use analytics to dominate the digital advertising industry. But support also comes from those who are sharply critical of what these companies are doing. For example, the noted critical journalist George Monbiot has made the case for deploying Big Data as an instrument to advance democracy. He has argued that analytics can be used to make political decision-making more transparent. Social movements can use the "wisdom of crowds" to expand democratic policy-making, to propose ideas that do not occur to professional politicians, and to find problems and loopholes in proposed legislation. In Monbiot's view, people will either control technology, or it will control them. I will have more to say about this in chapter six when the book turns to proposals for addressing the major social and political problems associated with the Next Internet. It is time to turn to what is arguably the most significant reason support for Big Data continues to grow, the third leg of the Next Internet: the Internet of Things.

BRINGING THINGS TO LIFE

The Internet of Things is a system for measuring, monitoring, and controlling the activity of objects and living organisms through sensors that gather, process, and report data over networks, including the Internet. From watches that measure blood pressure to refrigerators that tell us when we need more milk; from assembly lines worked by robots, to drones that deliver what robots produce, the Internet of Things promises a profound impact on individuals and society. We refer to the admittedly awkward term the Internet of Things because unlike the Internet we know, the Internet of Things electronically connects *things* in digital networks. The sensors in a refrigerator form a network in constant communication with a cloud data center. They might monitor food use and report to us, perhaps through a panel on the door, when we need to stock up again. The sensors that surround the body of a Tesla automobile form a network that scans the car's internal functioning and external environment in order to permit various degrees of autonomous driving. The Internet of Things is made possible by advances in the ability to miniaturize scanning devices and provide them with sufficient processing power to enable the ability to monitor activity, analyze data on their use, and deliver the results over electronic networks.

Most of what has been written about the Internet of Things is technical, promotional or both. Like most early analyses of new technological systems, it is satisfied to describe the technology, to encourage its use, and to situate the Internet of Things in utopian discourse. It is now hard to imagine an object that cannot literally contain a computer or enough computing power to warrant branding as an Internet of Things device. Those who have worked with digital scanning technologies are correct to point out that the Internet of Things is not an entirely new development in the information technology world. For the past 30 years, since the development of microprocessors and network-based instruments, companies in the oil and gas, chemical, pharmaceutical, manufacturing, and mining industries, have explored how to make use of sensors to make their business processes more efficient and safe. Unanticipated technological complexity leading to less than flawless operation and serious security issues (the Internet of Hackable Things is already an overused phrase), lead experts to advise that the Internet of Things is a slowly developing technology rather than the "killer app" that will instantly disrupt the world. Nevertheless, today's Internet of Things is qualitatively different because scanner costs continue to decline and because the limit on packing more computer power into devices has not been reached. The Internet of Things also benefits from the global digital networks that are now in place, and which continue to expand. Finally, the Internet of Things is significantly supported because of the opportunities for convergence with Cloud Computing and Big Data Analytics.

The term Internet of Things is not precisely accurate because the devices that comprise it also connect people. For example, the Apple Watch reports on its user's activity and sends to the user (and perhaps to other parties such as health authorities, insurance companies, and credit bureaus) information on the body's functioning and activities (steps walked in a day, heart rate, blood pressure, etc.) Some of these devices are actually embedded under the skin to improve health monitoring but implants are also intended to deepen surveillance as well. For example, a company in Sweden provides subcutaneous chips to its employees, removing the need for passwords to enter secure areas and to login to company sites. It also enables detailed performance monitoring. A firm in the United States markets a smart condom, which not only measures sexual activity, but it also claims to test for sexually transmitted disease. Another company is selling an app-enabled vibrator that can regulate and adjust sex toys from a phone or tablet (although it cost the company $5 million to settle a privacy lawsuit when a customer learned that the company was selling information on users without their informed consent). It is also the case that the Internet is not the only network for the Internet of Things. Companies and governments often make use of private networks with limited access and expanded security. Nevertheless, because the phrase Internet of Things is already in widespread use, it is best to go with it rather than add to the already long list of terms that fill descriptions of the online world.

The Internet of Things is also about the mundane, but powerful, economic and political demands of a global system. Whether global corporations are in the business of manufacturing things or providing services, their leaders see the Internet of Things as absolutely vital for their ability to produce more efficiently by expanding opportunities to add artificial intelligence to production facilities through so-called smart assembly lines, and robotics. They also imagine greater opportunities to distribute goods more efficiently and effectively at a lower cost. Not everyone will mimic Amazon's army of delivery drones, which the company expects will move goods to customers within 30 minutes of an order, but the principle of automated delivery, whether of clothes or university courses, provides a popular model for organizations in the twenty-first century. The opportunity to make more productive use of technology with many fewer workers makes the Internet of Things an essential consideration for organizations of every type, private and public, small and large, whether producing goods or delivering services.

The mere prospect of realizing this potential has greatly expanded the number of companies drawn to the opportunity to develop Internet of Things devices. The prospects for accelerating demand appear irresistible. Factories filled with robotic devices, scanners embedded all along assembly lines, and sensors monitoring industrial equipment like pumps, generators, motors, gauges, and switches comprise the industrial Internet of Things. These automated factories will increasingly produce the objects that make up the consumer Internet of Things whose driverless cars, intelligent homes, and biometric scanners, provide enormous opportunities to expand the sheer number of products on the market. There will be more things to want and more motivation to replace the things we like because smarter versions will constantly appear. The Internet of Things takes what used to be called planned obsolescence to entirely new levels. Create a small wand that can be passed over bar codes to ease the process of reordering and the two forces that often slow the consumption process, having to leave the home and facing a price label, practically disappear. In fact, in some cases consumers will not even need to "push now" because smart kitchens and laundry rooms will be programmed to automatically reorder. Wear a chip under your skin and you no longer need keys or passwords. The potential for self-monitoring is practically unlimited. In addition to the value of expanded consumer choice in goods and services, the Internet of Things massively increases the amount of valuable data gathered on consumers that can be sold to advertisers and other interested parties including, for example, insurance firms that provide medical and health coverage, credit bureaus that determine mortgage, auto, and other loan qualifications, and law-enforcement authorities monitoring citizen behavior (Table 1).

The Internet of Things emerges in a political as well and an economic context. Since 9/11 that means governments committed to vastly tightened security and strengthened intelligence gathering, all in the interest of fighting terrorism. So it is no surprise that governments everywhere are giving special attention to the massive new surveillance opportunities that the Internet of Things presents. Billions of interconnected devices monitoring the most minute activities of people and things can provide the National Security Agency (NSA), the Central Intelligence Agency (CIA), and their counterparts in other nations with what amounts to billions of new eyes

Table 1. Forecast Growth in the Number of Internet of Things Devices (in Billions).

2018: 23.1

2019: 26.7

2020: 30.7

2021: 35.8

2022: 42.6

2023: 51.1

2024: 62.1

2025: 74.4

Source: Forbes, November 22, 2016, http://bit.ly/2oLMkwz.

trained on people and institutions all over the world. Any human activity that makes use of a connected device and any process or practice of the businesses, government agencies, schools, and voluntary organizations that use the Internet of Things is trackable. So in addition to the efficiencies that the Internet of Things can bring to public agencies at every level, there is the specter of Big Brother and the seemingly insatiable appetite to gather, process, analyze, and use electronic surveillance.

For companies that provide Internet of Things services, mastery of the new technology of connected devices is absolutely vital for their growth, if not for their survival. These include the firms that are known around the world as leaders in the online world, such as Amazon, Microsoft, Google, Apple, and Facebook who, in their own different ways, are developing a strong Internet of Things presence within, and independent from, their social media strengths. The Internet of Things is especially critical for Amazon because, more than the others, the world's largest bookseller is now in the business of delivering a wide variety of goods. That is why Amazon is racing to develop consumer friendly digital assistants, robotic processing of warehouse orders, drone delivery, and new forms of packaging that automate reordering. The Internet of Things is also critical for older or legacy firms like General Electric and IBM that view the new technical system as an opportunity to retool their industrial base by expanding robotic production, taking advantage of enhanced scanning and monitoring capabilities, and making extensive use of Big Data Analytics.

With the growth of the Cloud and Big Data Analytics, the Internet of Things has a strong foundation upon which to build. The IT giant Cisco projects that 50 billion devices will be connected by 2020 and 82 billion by 2025, with the technology and services market reaching $14.4 trillion by 2022. Even if we discount the hyperbole that typically accompanies industry forecasts, these are, by any measure, massive growth expectations. Intel, using a broader definition of a device envisions 200 billion connected objects equipped with sensors and connectivity by the year 2020. Nevertheless, as Cisco also reports, there is a great deal of attrition in the Internet of Things market with three out of every four projects ending in failure.

It is easy to get lost in the mountain of terms and statistics that accompany promising new technologies like the Internet of Things. Before proceeding further down that road, it is useful to consider concrete examples of how successful companies are envisioning the future in this brave new world. Amazon leads the consumer Internet of Things and General Electric is arguably the major corporate power in industrial applications. Although its shareholders complain that the company is too eager to opt for new lines of business over expanding earnings, Amazon, by most measures, is one of the world's more successful companies. Most people are aware that it is a leader in mail order retailing but fewer know about its success in the post-Internet world of Cloud Computing where Amazon is widely recognized as the dominant player. Its cloud subsidiary Amazon Web Services controls over one-third of the market in the Public Cloud, the primary form of Cloud Computing, well ahead of its nearest competitor Microsoft with less than 20 percent market share. Amazon entered the cloud computing business because it stored customer information in data centers. The company decided to take advantage of its technological expertise selling cloud storage and extended that by offering value-added data processing. By combining this with its experience in retail discounting, Amazon was able to undercut the competition on price and rapidly rise to a dominant position.

The company has done the same with Big Data Analytics. From its early days, Amazon made use of analytics to assess and use the mountains of customer data it receives every day. Now Amazon is offering low-price data science, what it calls Amazon Machine Learning (AML), to customers, like small businesses, that might benefit from Big Data Analytics but cannot afford a full-service data science operation like IBM. AML is built on the same technology that Amazon uses to create algorithms that send book recommendations to email inboxes every day.

Amazon's vision of the consumer future begins with Alexa, a voice-operated digital assistant that responds to commands and carries out tasks such as turning on home lights, ordering music, and carrying out searches. This is complemented by the Dash button, a device about the size of a flash drive that appears on products and carries the logo of a product and a button. It is integrated into home Wi-Fi systems and, at the push of the Dash button, can reorder the product from Amazon for next day delivery to Amazon Prime customers. The company which pioneered one-click shopping on its website is also working with manufacturers to embed the Dash button in product packaging. In addition, Amazon is producing a device that can read bar codes for instant reordering of any product and with others, like Whirlpool, to automate the reordering process through the appliance itself. Think of an intelligent washing machine that orders its own detergent. The goal is to automate consumption. In the process, Amazon also collects massive amounts of information on its customers' everyday lives that the company uses in its own business and which it markets to companies wanting to know about customer tastes and shopping habits. Competitors recognize the threat and are responding. In May 2017, Walmart filed a patent for a sensor that the company would embed in all of its products to monitor consumer behavior, tighten inventory control and permit automatic reordering.

Once Alexa, Dash or their equivalent orders a product, attention shifts to Amazon's automated warehouse where robots, more like driverless vehicles, motor down "streets" to find, fetch, and deliver to a human "pick worker" the ordered product. The laborers who used to roam warehouses in search of products are no longer needed, at least not in nearly the same numbers. Their job now is mainly limited to lifting merchandise orders from a pod and placing them in a mailing box. Amazon expects that the process will soon be completed by automated delivery through an army of drones. Traveling at 50 MPH through airspace between 200 and 500 feet and weighing about 55 pounds, these flying delivery devices will carry packages weighing up to 5 pounds through travel corridors up to 10 miles long. Amazon's goal is to have drones complete delivery within 30 minutes of an order.

Automated ordering, automated order fulfillment, and automated delivery. This is Amazon's vision for the near future with the Internet of Things. Alexa is one of the company's most heavily marketed products ("Alexa," goes the commercial, as Dad reads to his child, "what sound does a whale make?"). Driverless vehicles are already operating in the warehouses; you can order a free (if you are an Amazon Prime customer) Dash device now (one click!); and the drones are in the test stages of development. What justifies such a massive investment is the enormous savings in labor costs, the likelihood that the easier it is to make a purchase, the more people will buy, and the more finely detailed data to be gathered on people's purchasing habits and used internally or sold to other companies. There is no guarantee that any or all of these systems will work well on their own or together to produce a seamless purchase–delivery process. Much can go wrong along the way to disturb the process, from hackers making digital mischief to the many errors that disrupt physical systems, not the least of which is the potential for drone failures. Yes, they test well in the wilderness of British Columbia but this is no guarantee they will work on the streets of Chicago. Nevertheless, the Amazon plan emphasizes just how close the world is coming to the deployment of Internet of Things technologies and, as subsequent chapters detail, just how essential it is to develop policies to deal with them.

When we turn to the industrial Internet of Things, it is useful to provide illustrations from General Electric, by today's standards an ancient company, but one that has remade itself many times over. On April 10, 2015 the then 123-year-old firm announced yet another makeover, this time finding its future in its past. As the banner headline in the *Financial Times* read: "GE to shed financial services arm in radical return to industrial roots." The move earned the attention because it marked a major retreat from the financial services sector, which, in the years leading up to the 2009 industry meltdown, dominated global capitalism. The company still brought in half of its earnings from its GE Capital unit, so selling off the unit and returning to its once core business of making jet engines, oil drilling equipment, and medical devices was no minor decision. However, returning to its industrial roots has nothing to do with factories filled with skilled assembly workers earning a union wage. Rather it means a manufacturing space that deploys robots, 3D printers, ubiquitous sensors, and massive connectivity with far fewer human beings in the mix than would populate most industrial plants in the twentieth century.

GE's iconic slogan used to be "We bring good things to life." Today, that phrase holds a deeper meaning because the company not only plans to once again bring things to life, it also plans to do so by bringing to life the very factories that build them. The company calls it the "brilliant factory," a manufacturing system whose machine parts communicate constantly with operators who can schedule maintenance before breakdowns occur and otherwise adjust the manufacturing process to changing conditions and fluctuating product demand. Factories have always been able to make adjustments, more in small batch than in larger production runs. But there is a qualitative difference in the agility of production when an assembly process contains 10,000 sensors that oversee and communicate instantly about the production of a battery in GE's Schenectady, New York plant. GE believes that the Industrial Internet of Things could add between $10 trillion to $15 trillion to global GDP by 2035 through more efficient and agile production, maintenance schedules that are fine-tuned to the specific materials that make up the manufacturing process, and lower cost repairs to industrial equipment. That would be the equivalent of adding another China or United States to the global economy.

Like the Cloud and Big Data Analytics, the Internet of Things faces major technical challenges. These include significant security issues. The Internet of what some call Hackable Things is vulnerable to breaches because producers, especially of Internet-enabled consumer devices, have been so eager to get their toys, watches, and thermostats to this highly competitive market that they have paid insufficient attention to software and data protection. Experts on the subject agree that there is almost no incentive for manufacturers to make their products secure because it is cheaper to sell them with minimal protection and then market new versions. That is why some industry people, to the surprise of observers, are calling for government regulation to prevent massive market failure. In the meantime, hackers have attacked individual devices and, more importantly, have mobilized large numbers of devices and ordered them to attack key network nodes. These "denial of service" attacks have crippled the networks of major providers by overloading their systems with demands from easily hackable thermostats, toys, and other Internet-enabled objects. In one such attack, hackers leveraged 2.5 million unsecured Internet of Things devices to target servers operated by a U.S. company providing domain name servers to several large and popular sites, including Netflix and Reddit. As a result, large portions of the Internet simply disappeared from view.

Moreover, consider that the billions of new online devices will require frequent software updates to remain secure and also to improve functionality. Many of these operations will be the responsibility of the consumer who is unlikely to have much interest in downloading an update to a teddy bear that can deliver music stored online. Companies will likely promote new teddy bears, thermostats, or watches because they contain the latest in secure software and added capability. Given how often people now buy new smart phones and other gadgets equipped with "the next new thing," however banal, firms are confident that customers will open their wallets for the devices equipped with 2.0 capabilities. However, this strategy is not without the risk of consumer fatigue and frustration that might tempt users to stash their Internet-enabled devices in the basements and attics that already contain numerous generations of what used to be their favorites, as they choose to return to a more analog life. The early signs of worry for the Internet of Things industry were evident by the first half of 2017 when it was reported that 75 percent of IOT projects had already ended in failure.

THE POWER AND PERIL OF CONVERGENCE

Cloud Computing, Big Data Analytics, and the Internet of Things each contain great technical power and potential. This power is multiplied when they are brought together or converge in the networks that comprise the Next Internet. The Cloud provides essential storage and processing; Big Data offers new opportunities for adding value to this stored information; and the Internet of Things collects mountains of data for analysis. Technological innovations, including work-place robotics, autonomous vehicles, and weaponized drones all require the tight integration of these three systems. Through their sensors, production-line robots are in constant communication with cloud data centers, which modify robot activities on the line based on performance indicators that undergo constant analytics review and whatever changes managers want to make in output specifications. No auto-mobile could drive without a human behind the wheel and no battlefield drone would be able to produce "bugsplat," the gruesome term pilots like to call their human prey, with-out a high degree of technological convergence.

Convergence is far easier to talk about than to achieve in practice. Technical systems that power the Cloud and the

Internet of Things require complex designs or architectures to enable their functioning, even as they protect themselves from external attacks. It is all the more difficult when these already complex systems try to achieve seamless interconnection. Having installed a Wi-Fi thermostat in my home, I learned just how difficult convergence can be when it stopped communicating with the data center servers that were to enable me to make changes in my home environment from an app on my phone. Having experienced a furnace shutdown that can lead to disaster in a Canadian winter, I installed the system to permit me to keep an eye on it when, like many other aging Canadians, I flee to the warm South in winter. Whether it was a data center outage, overloaded servers, a bad router, or faulty networks, I will never know. But for more than one frustrating month, the system was down more than it was up and running.

As the earlier discussion of Edge computing demonstrated, figuring out the proper relationship between devices and data centers is a big debate topic among those designing and building the Next Internet. Convergence is not just about interconnecting systems and enabling them to communicate. It also crucially concerns how to do this most effectively. In the relationship between cloud data systems and the Internet of Things, there are questions about whether the former is equipped to bear the demand that the proliferation of network-enabled devices will continue to generate. Companies continue to build data centers as the devices proliferate. Will there be sufficient data center capacity and will these information factories be able to respond quickly and efficiently enough to manage the host of complex sensor systems that have little tolerance for error? Some argue that more of the intelligence and management functions need to be shifted to the devices themselves with architectures designed to create local networks that rely less, if at all, on the Cloud. At the extreme, there are those who envision a significantly reduced role for cloud systems in Next Internet networks. Others maintain that the Cloud has worked well enough so far and will likely be able to take on generations of new devices. There is a great deal at stake here, not the least of which is the safety of autonomous vehicles that demand near instantaneous sensor response. Or the safety of the nuclear weapons arsenal.

There are, as yet, no clear answers and there may never be. Undoubtedly, adjustments will be made in the relationship between centralized servers and local devices for quite some time. However, what the debate does reveal is that convergence is more than a technical matter. It is not just about system architecture and design; it is also about the power relationships among companies that stand to gain or lose if one or another design path is chosen. Big investors in cloud computing facilities and services are counting on a massive boost in business as the Internet of Things advances. They do not want to see this expectation diminished or nullified by new architectures that take functionality from data centers and build it into the devices that foreshadow what some are already calling a "serverless future." In essence, technology, convergence, and the design of networks are not just a matter of applied science. As the next chapter emphatically concludes, politics plays a significant role in each.

More than the Cloud, Big Data Analytics, and the Internet of Things make up the Next Internet. Telecommunications systems connect these systems and their wired and wireless links are vital. Big providers like Verizon see the value in expanding beyond serving as distributors of valuable data and are getting into the action. This helps to explain the company's purchase of Yahoo, a once successful Internet company that still enjoys a following even though it has dipped in value well below the Big Five tech firms. Developments like this warrant close scrutiny, but so far telecommunications firms have not been particularly good at turning their network success into profitable Next Internet firms with a full set of Cloud Computing, Big Data Analytics, and Internet of Things services.

Telecommunications networks are important for convergence to succeed. However, even more important is a key element of convergence that tends to be ignored: the relationship between technical systems and human beings. Human–computer interaction has been an interest of scholars since the advent of the big, clunky word processors that initiated the personal computer era. In spite of rapid changes in systems, there was always something familiar about the relationship. After all, people had worked on typewriters for generations and so keyboards and even touch systems were not far from the human experience. Today's systems present a new set of challenges. The rise of intelligent devices, robotics, and artificial intelligence systems now means a different relationship to devices. Previous systems, however complex, tended to give users a large degree of control. That is no longer the case. Increasingly, people work alongside or as assistants to robots and other intelligent devices that are more critical to the production process. Increasingly, people give up most, if not all, control to autonomous vehicles and to the algorithms that are now trusted to make decisions in business, government, and social life. Human convergence, for more and more people, means subservience to the technologies and the algorithmic decision-making processes that make up the Next Internet. So much attention has been understandably paid to the concern that intelligent devices will lead to automation and the replacement of human workers that we tend to ignore the fact that most people, both at and away from work, will establish relationships, including strong emotional ones, with intelligent devices. What we are beginning to see with robotics and smart phones will only accelerate with the Next Internet. How this element of convergence does or does not work will go a long way to determining the success of the Next Internet and most likely, at the risk of sounding dramatic, very much of our future.

NOWHERE AND EVERYWHERE

Complicating matters is an ontological shift, a genuine change in the nature of those things we somewhat anachronistically call computers. What is a computer? Is it the device sitting on your desktop? Is it your laptop? Your tablet? Your smartphone? Your watch? Your thermostat? Your car, which now operates like a data center on wheels? It is increasingly difficult to determine what is and what is not a computer because computers appear to be everywhere. In addition to the power of the three systems described in this chapter, genuine ubiquity is a vital characteristic distinguishing the Internet as we now know it from its successor.

Another way to think about this is that digital is disappearing even as it becomes more powerful. The analogy to electricity is useful. When the technology that would power so much of the twentieth century appeared, there was no missing it because electricity required the presence of big, bulky generators on site. Combined with the appearance of transmission cables seemingly everywhere, it was impossible to ignore the presence of electricity. Over time, things changed. The generators were centralized, the cables were buried (at least in most urban areas) underground, and the wires disappeared into the woodwork. Electricity lost visibility, even as it became more powerful. It is not precisely the same for digital because digital is not quite intelligent electricity. However, the analogy is worth considering because it appears that, as digital is becoming as ubiquitous as electricity, it too is disappearing into the wood-work of everyday life. We once viewed electricity as a thing outside ourselves, embodied in very material technologies obviously external to the people who used them. Similarly we once viewed computers as contained within material machines external to their users. Whether it was a mainframe, a work-station, a personal computer, a tablet, or a smartphone, we knew a computer when we saw it. It was external to and clearly distinguishable from us. That is no longer the case.

Not quite ubiquitous, computers are nevertheless increas-ingly embedded in so many devices and bodies, including our own, that they appear to be everywhere, yet nowhere in particular. This represents at least the beginning of an onto-logical shift in the nature of these devices. Less a thing out there and more a characteristic of most everything we con-front, including ourselves, the arrival of what was once called ubiquitous computing is also a form of convergence. In this case, computers converge with the world as we know it, including objects, people, and nature itself. Computational power is increasingly derived from its presence nearly every-where, marking another significant difference between the Next Internet and its predecessor. Another significant differ-ence is the political economic context that shapes this power, a topic taken up in the next chapter.

CHAPTER 3

POWER, POLITICS AND POLITICAL ECONOMY

It's not populism that we should fear; it is totalitarian capitalism and it's coming to a website near you.
— Carl Mortished

TECHNOLOGY AND POWER

The last chapter ended with a reference to computational power. It is common to think of technology and power by assessing the capabilities of the former to bring about changes in people, their institutions, and in other things. We think of the power of a data center to store information, the power of Big Data Analytics to find needles of understanding in haystacks of raw data, and the power of the Internet of Things to bring devices to life by helping people to manage their lives and by promoting the benefit of an "always on" relationship to digital devices. When it comes to power we tend to reify technology, giving it human-like qualities. While the value of thinking about technology and power in this way is certainly understandable, if only as a shorthand for a more complex explanation, this chapter challenges it by examining the power structure represented primarily by the corporations and government institutions that shape the production, distribution, and use of digital technology.

I view politics in the political economy sense, which seeks to understand the social relations, particularly the power relations, that mutually constitute the production, distribution, and of resources, in this case, media, information, and communication resources. In essence, power involves the ability to reach a goal in the face of human and technical obstacles. If you can get what you want even when others do not want you to get it, then you can be said to have power. My approach to political economy here focuses especially on the process of commodification, which examines the transformation of goods and services valued for their uses into things or commodities that are valued for what they can bring in the marketplace. When I tell my granddaughter a story from my childhood, I am valuing the story for its use in entertaining her and letting her know about her family. If I were to sell the story to a publisher for a fee, then it would go through a process of commodification that creates exchange value. The Next Internet expands and accelerates the commodification process by increasing the world's information storage and processing capacity in cloud data centers, by increasing the ability to add value to information through Big Data Analytics, and through the manifold growth in data collected by Internet of Things devices. It also expands opportunities to commodify users by marketing their identities and attention to advertisers and other interested organizations, and similarly enlarges the potential to commodify the labor of those employed in and around the tech industry.

FROM RESEARCH TO COMMERCE

When the original Internet arrived, there was not much indication that it would evolve into a fully commercial system. That was because it was born and grew up under the tutelage of government agencies and in the shadow of a government-mandated breakup of the largest telecommunications company in the United States. The first of the two key government agencies was the Defense Advanced Research Projects Agency, an arm of the U.S. military, which carried out studies on new technologies that might have military applications. With deep pockets and a broad mandate, DARPA also funded external research from practical applications to what one computer historian calls "pie-in-sky" ideas, which might lead nowhere but which also might open entirely new opportunities in military technology. In the 1960s and 1970s, DARPA-funded research led to a key to long-distance data communication, packet switching, a system for breaking up messages into digital packets for efficient transmission and reassembly at the point of reception. The military was especially interested in this digital tool because it enabled flexible transmission over multiple networks, a key to effective combat communication. Permitting communication over vast distances between computers, with little to no human intervention, packet switching was an enormous advance over existing telecommunications networks. DARPA-funded research at universities and private research organizations like Bolt, Baranek and Newman, honed the development of packet switching and also led to file sharing, email, and other building blocks of the original Internet. Working mainly with university researchers who were interested in expanding digital communication among scientists, the agency led the way until 1985 when management of the emerging system was turned over to another government agency, this time it was the civilian National Science Foundation.

NSF funneled government money to support basic and applied research primarily at universities. It also managed the burgeoning digital communication networks with the primary purpose of enabling the research community in the United States to work cooperatively. Specifically, it helped to scale up the national network by involving more research facilities and especially by expanding the use of supercomputer facilities whose large fixed cost raised questions about government funding priorities. Crucially, the NSF also gave its blessing to a set of standards for digital networks that had been developed by DARPA. The TCP/IP protocol, which stands for transmission control protocol and Internet protocol, defined the method for sending and receiving data through packet switched networks. It remains in use today. By 1989 the NSFNET had provided researchers across the country with a taste for "inter-networking," a term that was eventually shortened to Internet.

All of this took place in the context of the greatest transformation in the history of the U.S. telecommunications industry, what came to be called the breakup of AT&T, the American Telephone and Telegraph Corporation, also known as the Bell System. The company was, until 1982, the country's monopoly provider of telephone service and one of its major employers, with workers in every city, town, and, significantly for politics, every congressional district. For years the company maintained an economic and political equilibrium by providing near universal telephone service and full-time, unionized work to generations of men and women in return for a guaranteed profit and regulatory protection against the threat of competition. But it was equilibrium for an era of wired analog telephony and, although it tried, AT&T could not fend off the forces supporting technological change. These were led by large business users, including banks, energy companies, and the growing array of transnational businesses, all demanding the latest technology, including digital computer-to-computer communication systems. They also wanted the lowest possible rates. If that required opening the telecommunications and new data services markets to competition, then so be it. Alongside corporate America, a growing array of consumer organizations, led by the well-known advocate Ralph Nader, mobilized to fight the Bell monopoly.

In addition to its workforce, led by the powerful Communication Workers of America union, AT&T enjoyed the support of the Department of Defense, which could count on the company to provide the customized services required by the military and which was less constrained than private businesses and individual consumers by price considerations. After years of political wrangling, including Federal Communications Commission hearings on the computer industry beginning in the 1960s and a Justice Department suit against AT&T initiated in 1974, the parties came to an agreement that took effect in 1984. Once the deal received the blessing of the Defense Department, it was just a matter of finalizing details that would see the company broken up into seven regional Bell companies and a long-distance carrier retaining the name AT&T. Of vital importance for developing data networks, the regional companies were not permitted to offer products and services in competitive markets like computer and information services. AT&T and its manufacturing arm Western Electric were permitted to do so, as was IBM, once the government dropped an antitrust action against the computer manufacturer. With the telephone giant cut down to size and IBM on notice that the government was keeping a close eye on its anti-competitive practices, emerging services that would ultimately comprise the Internet were free to develop in a decentralized environment. This enabled a variety of government, commercial, and non-governmental organizations to experiment with the new technologies of digital communications without fear that AT&T or any of the regional telephone companies would resort to the monopoly practices that once blocked competitors from connecting their telephones to the AT&T system.

One consequence of these policy decisions was to make the NSF more comfortable with the decision to begin privatizing the NSFNET in 1989, just when Tim Berners-Lee was publishing his first paper on how to make the new networked data communication systems available to anyone with access to networks anywhere in the world. However, it also meant that the U.S. government would not take steps to create a publicly owned and managed national data communication system nor one that, while private, might be regulated according to the public interest principles that had governed telecommunications and broadcasting. The visions of a public computer utility that had emerged in some expert discussions beginning in the 1960s were set aside. There would be no mandate for universal access at affordable rates, no equivalent of a fairness doctrine to govern political speech, no controls on advertising, and no provisions for licensing carriers based on their ability to serve the public equitably and ethically. There is little doubt that the NSF decision sped up technological development, but it also opened the door to many of today's problems, especially in the use of social media. Moreover, it did so for the entire world without consultation and certainly without negotiation. Because the United States was first off the mark with new systems of computer-based data communication, decisions to privatize and commercialize established patterns and precedents would be very difficult for other nations to overturn. For example, every attempt to empower the United Nations, particularly through the

International Telecommunication Union, an agency put in place to make decisions when the telegraph was new, has failed to accomplish anything meaningful because the United States resists genuine global governance of what amounts to a global means of communication.

At the time, the primary consequence of these developments for the Internet was that no single entity would dominate. Not that anyone tried. There was so much uncertainty about the commercial potential in new data networks that none of the big firms tried to become the Internet's version of AT&T. The uncertainty is characteristic of the marketplace in new technological systems, including early radio, whose commercial potential took years to figure out. As a result, as networks emerged, including the network of networks we have come to call the Internet, potential participants warily experimented without major commitments. These included traditional media companies, new businesses, government agencies, universities, amateur enthusiasts, political activists, and others. They used several different networks, each operating with slightly different standards that in the late 1980s and early 1990s lurched toward compatibility and convergence around the TCP/IP Internet standard. The complex mix of organizations, technologies, and approaches operating in an environment of some promise and great uncertainty, especially about commercial potential, fed visions of building a communication system that would expand democracy and undermine all forms of authoritarianism. Participation in public life would grow. Social divisions would diminish. Education and health care would find a new partner to deliver services to all, irrespective of location and income.

As technologists worked on engineering the Internet, the wide range of participants worked on a vision that began by imagining a society where information is fully accessible to all citizens as an essential service. In this vision, information is managed through forms of regulation and control that are governed by representative institutions whose goal is the fullest possible access and control for the greatest number of citizens. Governance might take multiple forms, including different combinations of centralized and decentralized approaches at local, regional, national, and international levels. Today, with the emergence of the Next Internet, this vision is in decline and a new one is emerging. The second envisions a world controlled by global corporations and the surveillance and intelligence arms of national governments. Under this model, the market is the leading force shaping decisions about the production, distribution and exchange of information, and corporations with market power hold the most influence. In this fundamentally undemocratic world, digital behemoths share power with governments that make full use of technology for surveillance, control, and coercion. We now face the question of whether this tendency can be reversed and whether it is possible to return to the earlier vision of a genuinely public and democratic Next Internet.

BIG TECH

What is the political economy that is giving rise to this darker vision? I begin with corporations that comprise the Next Internet power structure and then turn to the government agencies whose influence helps to shape power in the digital world. The industry that brings together the Cloud, Big Data, and the Internet of Things is quite complex with dominant firms, legacy companies, startups, upstarts, disrupters, specialists, and generalists. Amid the complexity, five corporations stand out for their financial value, their influence across all three Next Internet systems, and for their overwhelming control over one or more of Cloud Computing, Big Data

Analytics, and the Internet of Things. These include, in order of market capitalization: Apple, Google, Microsoft, Amazon, and Facebook. Table 2 tells an interesting story about their rise to riches. On August 1, 2016, for the first time, five companies from the same industry led the world in market value. Gone from the top were the energy and financial services companies. Gone were the giants from Russia and China. American Big Tech clearly led the world. Market

Table 2. The Five Largest Firms in the World by Market Value in $Billions US.

August 1, 2006	
Exxon	$413B
GE	$336B
Microsoft	$245B
Gazprom	$244B
Citigroup	$240B
August 1, 2011	
Exxon	$392B
Apple	$368B
PetroChina	$298B
ICBC	$240B
Shell	$229B
August 1, 2016	
Apple	$571B
Alphabet (Google)	$540B
Microsoft	$441B
Amazon	$364B
Facebook	$357B

Source: Bloomberg, August 2, 2016 http://bloom.bg/2b8mfm5.

capitalization can change from day to day and, along with it, corporate rankings. Nevertheless, there is something quite extraordinary in the dominance of these five firms. As of June 2017 their dominance persisted with no change in the rankings at the top of the market cap list.

Each of the Big Tech Five is a diverse firm with investments in all three Next Internet systems. But each achieved hegemony in a specific business. Apple exploited its design capabilities to capture the hardware market particularly in the booming smartphone business. It has considerable experience in the Cloud where it stores data generated by its proprietary email, music, video, photo, and messenger services. Customers are also offered a pay-for-storage service, iCloud, for customers who want to keep their own files in the data centers of the company that sells them hardware and services. Big Data Analytics is in continuous use to thoroughly assess and constantly market new content and services to customers through carefully designed interfaces like the online iTunes store and its Apple Music subscription service. Unlike Amazon, Microsoft, and Google, which are leaders in the Public Cloud, Apple provides Cloud and analytics almost exclusively to its own customer base. Also unlike these companies, it has created a closed architecture with its own operating system and apps that connect an Apple community of users. Apple has also invested heavily in the Internet of Things with its intelligent wristwatch leading the way and its focus on gathering data on our bodies making it a leader in promoting the quantified and commodified self. Worried about concentrating too heavily on the iPhone, Apple has also bet on creating its own digital assistant, the HomePod. It has also invested substantially in autonomous vehicle technology. However, so much secrecy and uncertainty surrounds the project that it is hard to determine whether the company will actually join the growing list of significant players.

Nevertheless, with about $250 billion in cash invested in long-term securities that is not counted against net worth, Apple is expected to soon become the world's first trillion-dollar company.

Unlike Apple, which concentrated on hardware, Google, also known as Alphabet, the holding company that owns Google, built its empire by teaching people how to search online and by selling advertising customized to user search patterns. As a result, along with Facebook, the company controls two-thirds of the digital advertising market and an astounding 85 percent of all new digital advertising dollars, a major source of funding for most online media. Its monopoly over search ad revenue stood at 88 percent in 2017. In the United Kingdom, where a similar oligopoly holds, the Press Gazette, a publication representing journalists, has mounted a campaign to break up the Facebook–Google duopoly, quite correctly maintaining that the British government would not tolerate such domination in two newspapers.

The company that began by proclaiming that it would not take commercial advertising because ads would compromise its ethical standards has now deployed the model across its online properties, including Gmail, Google News, and YouTube. Today, the space accompanying Google queries is the Internet's most valuable real estate for ads.

In the years since Google began to place advertising above search results, the company has incrementally allocated more space to advertisements and expanded the forms they take. The result is called ad creep and it has pushed standard or unpaid search results farther down the screen, an effect even more noticeable on smaller smartphone screens.

Its ad-driven business has given Google the largest and most powerful commercial Cloud. However, because it was built to serve users of its own services, the Google Cloud is not easily adapted to the needs of new customers, especially large businesses. To remedy this, the company is investing $10 billion a year in Cloud Computing in the hope of catching industry leaders Amazon Web Services and Microsoft's Azure cloud service. Google has invested heavily in data analytics and in the Internet of Things. The former primarily serves its advertising clients with detailed profiles on users, but it also does serious data mining for research on social trends. One of the reasons for creating the holding company Alphabet was to distinguish revenue generators like Google search from research activities into new products such as autonomous vehicles. It also intended to market these capabilities to other firms interested in developing their own Internet of Things products. Of special interest to the company is its stake in artificial intelligence through its Deep Learning project. As institutions make more use of AI, Google hopes to package Deep Learning with its cloud computing products. Moreover, to counter the efforts of telecommunications companies to edge their way into the space occupied by Google, the company has built a private fiber optic cable network that reaches 33 countries.

Although not as rich as Apple, Google is arguably more diversified and therefore more likely to sustain the inevitable changes that regularly buffet technology markets. Over the past five years, it has become the dominant technology company in American education. Along with other tech firms like Facebook, it aims to massively expand the role of technology in schools, diminish the power of teachers, and create lifelong customers. To do so, Google has recruited educators and administrators to promote its own hardware, especially the Chromebook, and software, including Gmail and apps tailored for the classroom, to other schools. It uses teachers to test its products, with or without the knowledge of school districts. Once dominant in the classroom, Apple can no longer hold a candle to Google for pre-eminence at all levels of education. Fully half of all students in the United States use Gmail and other Google software, which the company expects will win them customers for life. Once floundering Chromebooks now account for half of all mobile devices shipped to American classrooms. Google is also a major force behind the organization Code.org, which has expanded its hold on school curricula by promoting the teaching of code at every level of schooling. At the higher education level, Google supports a massive university research program that pays professors $5,000 to $400,000 for studies that defend the company in areas where its business practices are questioned in the press or where it faces regulatory challenges. The issue attracted significant media attention in 2017 when it was learned that many of the grant recipients failed to disclose their financial relationship to the company.

Unlike Apple and Google, Microsoft has maintained its position among the top five by building on its near monopoly over computer operating systems to become the world leader in word processing, spread sheet, and presentation software. In a major change for the company, its customers, and competitors, Microsoft has integrated these products into its Azure cloud computing business, making them available online for a subscription fee. This provides the company with enormous leverage because customers no longer purchase software outright but must rely on, and pay, Microsoft on a continuing basis. Moreover, by bundling software with cloud storage, the company has used its widely distributed products to become the second largest cloud computing business. Recognizing that more of its growth potential lies in the Cloud, Microsoft is investing heavily and restructuring its workforce to make the Cloud its focus. To emphasize the connection between concentrating on the Cloud and labor cost savings, the company announced in mid-2017 that preparations for the next push to the Cloud would be accompanied by eliminating 4,000 employees worldwide.

Microsoft also departs from other cloud computing companies, particularly the leader Amazon, by collaborating with partners to provide more than storage or basic services. For example, it has joined up with the aircraft manufacturing company Boeing to create and run aviation software in its Cloud. Some of these specialty projects involve building collaborations by bringing together its cloud and Internet of Things offerings. For example, Microsoft is working with the $13 billion agribusiness Land O'Lakes to analyze satellite imagery through its artificial intelligence service Azure Machine Learning in the hopes of boosting crop yields. In a portent for the future direction of agribusiness, the precise amount of seed per square meter was accurately determined and the information was downloaded to semi-autonomous vehicles that completed the planting. The result was an increase in yields from 130 bushels per acre prior to the partnership to 500 bushels. Microsoft is also making use of its expertise in the Cloud, Big Data, and the Internet of Things to help BMW and Renault-Nissan to develop autonomous vehicles.

Observing how well Microsoft makes use of its long history in the computer business, it is all the more remarkable that Amazon, with far less experience, has become the unquestioned global leader in Cloud Computing. Starting off as one of many online retailers, most of which fell victim to the dotcom crash that marked the start of this century, Amazon's founder Jeff Bezos consistently resisted shareholder pressure to boost earnings and instead zealously invested to build and diversify its e-commerce business. The company's clear monopoly over the e-book market, where in 2017 it controlled 74 percent of the sector, provided an excellent base from which to grow new businesses. Expansion required massive increases in facilities, from warehouses to stock the books and the other growing product lines its customers demanded to the data warehouses that processed orders and collected enough customer data to enable Amazon to precisely market to customers and build what has become a fiercely loyal following. Mastering the burgeoning field of digital logistics, Amazon came to understand that the company was in the information business as much as it was a retailer of material goods. This mastery of digital logistics and marketing has led the company to believe that there is practically no industry that it cannot disrupt and control. This includes the notoriously low margin grocery business, which Amazon attacked powerfully in 2017 when it spent $13.4 billion to purchase the popular, upscale company Whole Foods.

Much of the company's success, certainly its turn to profitability, stems from the 2006 formation of Amazon Web Services, the company's cloud provider. AWS has grown to capture one out of every three cloud computing dollars and earns revenues of $13 billion a year. With a global network of data centers serving its own customers and offering data storage to individuals and institutions, Amazon has mastered the Cloud and Big Data Analytics. AWS boasts more than one million customers, including McDonald's, Netflix, Airbnb, Adobe, Capital One, GE, Pinterest, and the Central Intelligence Agency. Moreover, Amazon is pioneering in the business use of Internet of Things devices including robotics to facilitate warehouse product fulfillment and drone delivery. The latter is a risky proposition that has some experienced IT experts scratching their heads. But heads were scratched when Amazon decided to become a cloud computing company well before most of its current cloud competitors who continue to play catch up. So it would not be surprising if Amazon customers had their latest order for

Cheerios breakfast cereal (I know an Amazon Prime customer who buys breakfast this way) delivered to their homes by drone. Moreover, Amazon adds to its revenue stream by selling cloud customers access to the machine learning capabilities that it uses to develop algorithms to forecast user behavior.

Even as it launches into the outer reaches of the digital world, Amazon distinguishes itself from the rest of the major Next Internet companies by investing in traditional media, even those expected to be left behind in the wake of technological change. Most prominently, Amazon's Jeff Bezos purchased the failing *Washington Post* newspaper. Once a leading voice in American politics, the *Post* fell on the hard times that have hit newspapers across the Western world. Bezos did not just buy the venerable D.C. daily, he helped to revive it by hiring large numbers of journalists at a time when most print outlets were letting them go. Moreover, unlike what happens when conservative or libertarian business moguls buy media, Bezos has at least tolerated, if not supported, the strengthening of the *Post's* progressive voice that has made it one of the fiercest critics of the Trump regime. Moreover, Amazon Studios has distinguished itself in television and film. In 2015 its hit television comedy-drama Transparent, which chronicles how a family came to terms with the knowledge that the person they thought was the family patriarch was actually transgender, won the Golden Globe award for Best Series. It was the first major win for a streaming media service. Amazon Studios has done even better in film with such award winners as Manchester by the Sea and 2017's recipient of the Academy Award for Best Foreign Film, The Salesman. The company's cloud division is even having a significant impact on the sport known as America's pastime, Major League Baseball. In a deal with the league, Amazon Web Services is providing this already statistics obsessed sport with data and analytics services that are reshaping the way the game is played and how it is televised. The latter is best exemplified in the constant references to esoteric data like the speed a batted ball reaches when it leaves the park for a home run and the angle of elevation of a hitter's swing. All of which, it is repeated again and again, is brought to the viewer by Amazon Web Services.

The power of Facebook starts from its dominant position in social media. With two billion users worldwide, the company has grown from a Harvard College project for students to learn about one another (and perhaps date) to become the largest online community in the world and the dominant distributor of news, both real and fake. Facebook and its subsidiaries Instagram, WhatsApp, and Messenger controlled 77 percent of mobile media traffic in 2017. Almost all of its valuation comes from the advertising market for its users whose free labor provides the profiles, posts, and photos that attract companies looking to pitch their products and services. We are Facebook's primary asset. Over the years, this process has been expanded with deepening electronic connections between users and advertisers. Now, in addition to ads appearing on user pages, including its email Messenger service, customized to user profiles, they also show up corresponding to what users do on other sites, including the credit card purchases they make to reveal advertising effectiveness. Clicks help to reveal preferences, but purchases seal the deal. Facebook continues to build data centers to store profiles but has not chosen to follow Amazon by selling cloud storage and services to other companies. Rather, evidenced by its purchases of Instagram, the photo posting company with over 700 million users, and the texting firm WhatsApp, with 1.2 billion users in 180 countries, Facebook plans to deepen the company's already firm leadership in global mobile services. The company has also made a major foray into Internet of

Things technologies by placing a big bet on the future of virtual reality systems with the acquisition of the VR firm Oculus.

The power of the Big Five in the tech world is unquestioned and its impact on national economies and governments, not the least through its influence on journalism, is profound. Their financial value surpasses that of most countries and their lobbying power, which only a few years ago was considered weak, is now a powerhouse in Washington, D.C. and in other world capitals. Google leads the way, spending more on lobbying than any other corporation, about $6 million, in the second quarter of 2017, on pace to spend about $25 million for the year. Amazon and Apple also broke their own records for lobbying in the first three months of 2017. The Big Five has used this power to master the global political economy, including keeping revenue away from tax authorities like those in the United States, by sheltering it in tax havens.

The Big Five controls and benefits from a global division of labor whose human cost is rarely captured in the logistics charts that map the world economy. Much attention is paid to the lavish working conditions their own employees enjoy in Silicon Valley and Seattle where most research, design, and engineering work takes place. However, these workers comprise a small fraction of those directly involved in the production process. Work actually begins in places like the coltan mines of the Democratic Republic of the Congo where workers using their own hands and primitive tools suffer some of the most hideous working conditions. They earn a pittance to dig for the mineral that Apple uses in the iPhone, Samsung in its Galaxy, and which is essential to many other devices and systems that power the Next Internet. Moreover, the fight to control revenue from the mines has fueled a bloody 20-year war.

Most of the Next Internet's hardware is actually built in East Asia, South Korea, and China where the Taiwanese company Foxconn and other contractors and sub-contractors for the major U.S. firms operate large factory complexes that resemble the company towns of the early industrial era. Employees live in crowded dormitories and eat at company cafeterias. They toil for long hours at low pay and encounter hazardous conditions that include numerous toxic substances to manufacture devices, including cloud data center servers and the many consumer devices that communicate with them. Suffering from the exhaustion that would understandably accompany a 70-hour or longer workweek, many employees suffer from neurological and respiratory disorders emanating from the dangerous chemicals they are exposed to all day. What has been called the "Iron Triangle" rules high tech production: ever-higher product value, ever-accelerating production speeds, and ever-cheaper production costs. Record-breaking market capitalizations do not come without a price that today is paid dearly by workers who mine essential rare metals in Africa, who make iPhones in the sweatshops of China, and who labor in American warehouses where Amazon employees fill orders that the company promises its best customers will be delivered the next day. High profit margins enable Big Tech firms to pay their professional staff in the United States very well and profits that are not reinvested in the company often take another logistics turn to the tax havens of countries eager court the lords of the Next Internet.

Powerful as they are now, each of these companies has known failure. Apple hit rock bottom in September 1996 and most analysts expected it to fold or be purchased for the value of its software. Almost no one expected the company to remain a hardware producer. The return of Steve Jobs, the creation of the iPod and then, most successfully, the iPhone, left skeptics eating their words. Yet, even now, there is concern about the growth potential in the phone market, and in the demand for tablets and watches. Moreover, Apple arrived late to the digital assistant competition and its entry into the driverless car sweepstakes appears to have been a rather bumpy ride. Google had great hopes for wiring the United States and the world with Google Fiber, but very little has come of its trials. Around for longer, Microsoft has littered the history of modern computing with its failures, including a web browser, a music player, a (not very) smartphone, clunky versions of its operating system, and poor deals, like the $8 billion it spent on Nokia. Amazon produced a short-lived phone, a travel service (how many now remember Destinations?), money products like Amazon Wallet and Web-Pay, and a high-end shopping service. Finally, Facebook has given us a failed real-time news app, an app creator, a home page for Android phones, a Groupon look-a-like deal service, an online shop for Facebook users, an email platform, a Snapchat look-a-like called Poke, and a variety of other unsuccessful, mainly copycat services.

Failures aside, the top five companies in technology enjoy extraordinary power over the development of the Next Internet. The structure and operation of the industry are also influenced by legacy firms, as well as by businesses that specialize in particular facets of the post-Internet world. Legacy companies are once dominant firms that retain power but have declined from upper tier status. Good examples of these include Intel, IBM, and Verizon. But before turning to these firms, it is important to consider arguably the biggest anomaly in the industry, General Electric, otherwise known as the 125-year-old startup.

CHALLENGERS TO THE BIG FIVE

With the exception of its ownership of the broadcasting company NBC at various stages in its history, General Electric has mainly manufactured products for the consumer and business electronics market. All that changed in 1997 when the company followed the power shift from industrial to finance capital by transforming itself into an investment company led by the newly created GE Capital. After a decade of success in the money business, the company got caught up in the turmoil of the global financial crisis. Determined to resist the constraints imposed by renewed financial sector regulation, the company decided to once again reinvent its core business. By 2009 it had completed the sale of GE Capital and turned to software and the industrial Internet of Things. The company that brought "good things to life" with light bulbs would now do so through code by enabling its own factories and those of its clients to deploy robots, artificial intelligence, and the full panoply of digital sensors to apply fully connected systems to the production, distribution, sale and maintenance of all things industrial. Starting with what the company calls "predictive maintenance," a sensor-driven early warning system that lessens the need for major retooling, the company plans to apply Next Internet tools to production lines worldwide. This strategy is not without major risks. Radically transforming a core business is never easy. Doing it twice in two decades is extraordinary. But GE is convinced that by taking the lead in a market that none of the Big Five has directly controlled, the industrial Internet of Things, it has an opportunity to upset their entrenched power.

Most legacy firms find it too risky to follow GE's pattern of reinvention. They choose instead to settle for maintaining a position that generates revenue even if that means giving up on reaching the stratosphere of the top five Next Internet companies. As the primary producer of the semiconductor chips and microprocessors that enabled the global spread of computer power, Intel has been an indispensable force since it was founded in 1968. Today the company continues to earn significant revenue by selling chips to the primary producers of the low-cost computers many use to navigate the Internet as we know it, including other legacy firms like Dell, Lenovo (formerly IBM's personal computer division and now a Chinese firm), and Hewlett-Packard. However, Intel has not significantly diversified its core business and its market capitalization is less than half that of Facebook and less than a third of Apple. Nevertheless, the company continues to actively make adjustments to maintain its relevance in the digital world, most notably in 2017 by spending $15.3 billion to purchase one of the largest producers of sensor and camera equipment for autonomous vehicles. Such purchases are part of a trend among legacy firms that use the strategy in an attempt to play catch-up with the giants. Limitations aside, Intel is in a good position to benefit from the surging demand for Internet of Things devices. Producing the chips that give self-driving cars and industrial robots their brains, that help servers analyze large datasets and that determine how fast a smartphone can manage texts, calls, and videos, Intel and other leading companies like Samsung, Qualcomm, and Toshiba will likely do well even if they are not, as one commentator contended "at the front line of Silicon Valley's biggest battles today."[3]

The major telecommunications firm Verizon's purchase of Yahoo reflects the inability of key players in a once dominant industry to keep pace with the Big Five. The world economy is littered with the failures of an industry once considered cutting edge. They may not have been considered household names but Ericsson, Nokia, Siemens, Nortel, WorldCom,

Enron, and Blackberry were once dominant in the way that the Big Five are today and they were expected to remain that way for years to come. Verizon, originally created from the merger of Bell Atlantic and GTE, is one of the more successful of the survivors but remains valued at well below the Big Five. The purchase of Yahoo represents its biggest bet on building a Next Internet presence and it is a risky one for various reasons, not the least of which is that Yahoo has a terrible track record for security. Well over a billion of its accounts have been breached. For this, Verizon made Yahoo accept a $350 million cut in its announced purchase price of $4.8 billion. Verizon should have demanded more because in March 2017, in spite of several arrests of Yahoo hackers, one billion of the hacked accounts remained on sale. Nevertheless, the Trump Administration provided Verizon with a major gift when it agreed to roll back privacy protections that the Obama government put in place to prevent Internet Service Providers like Verizon from selling information on its customers to advertisers. The opportunity to market a user's web browsing history without receiving permission provides an enormous boost to its bottom line and places Verizon on a level playing field with Google and Facebook, whose use of browser history for financial gain is not restricted.

After selling its personal computer division to the Chinese firm Lenovo in 2004, IBM has focused on the business market. Valued at somewhere between Intel and Verizon, it has succeeded in adding pieces to this strategy, such as the 2016 purchase of Truven, a leader in health analytics. This approach of adding relatively small companies (Truven cost IBM $2.6 billion) that fit IBM's very specific focus may prove more profitable, if less dramatic, than that of Verizon, whose purchase of Yahoo is eerily reminiscent of the failed merger of AOL and Time-Warner in 2001. These examples demonstrate the challenges that legacy firms face in trying to climb the Next Internet power structure or even to simply maintain their current position. They are not alone. The Cloud has disrupted many of the big names in information technology, including Cisco, Hewlett-Packard, and Oracle which succeeded by providing hardware, software, and services to corporate IT departments. As banks, insurance companies, energy businesses, governments, and other large institutional users downsize their own IT departments and move to the Cloud, there is less need for traditional IT services. As a result, these and other IT providers have had to make major adjustments in their core strategies, all of which involve a move to the Cloud. Given the power of the Big Five, this is no easy matter. Consider Oracle, which continues to do well but still relies on the declining business of servicing the needs of traditional IT departments. In 2016 on-premise revenues accounted for 67 percent of total revenues, a drop of a mere three percent from the previous year. In spite of its goal to shift its strategy, Cloud Computing accounted for only 13 percent of total sales. Legacy media companies are also pursuing their own digital strategies, evidenced by NBCUniversal's major investment in the parent company of the very successful Snapchat online photo, video, and messaging app. Snapchat's market cap, even discounting for a dive after its initial public offering, surpasses that of Twitter which stood at about $13 billion in June 2017.

The final group to consider comprises specialty companies that emerged with Cloud Computing and continue to depend on providing cloud services for most of their business. Salesforce, Workday, and Rackspace represent three good examples. They each offer opportunities to outsource IT and other major business functions to the Cloud. For example, Salesforce is a $59 billion company that specializes in managing customer relations. Companies turn to Salesforce to store data on marketing, sales and customer service in the Cloud and make use of its software and data analytics to carry out these functions more effectively and with less staff. Workday does the same for finance and human relations functions. Both Salesforce and Workday have succeeded because they have found specialized niches in the Next Internet arena. Rackspace started out successfully and became an industry leader in the all-purpose provision of cloud computing storage and services. However, its standing has been eroded by Amazon, Microsoft, and Google, which have been able to use their vast resources to continuously cut prices and provide general services that Rackspace and other cloud companies like it are not able to match. As a result, Rackspace hangs on but only because it has partnered with the Google Cloud and with the investment of a private equity firm that may eventually carve up and sell off the company. Given the power of the Big Five, and especially its three major cloud business providers, the only way for companies that grew with the Cloud to continue to prosper is by concentrating on specialized Next Internet services.

This trip through the structure of the U.S. Next Internet industry demonstrates the power of its top five companies and indeed of the entire U.S. digital technology industry. Scholars and policy observers used to debate the consequences of a world dominated by American media until the media in Europe and throughout the developing world came to challenge that hegemony. Now as the Cloud, Big Data Analytics, and the Internet of Things converge to form the Next Internet, it is once again American companies that appear dominant.

GOVERNMENT EMBRACES THE NEXT INTERNET

American power is reinforced by the U.S. government and particularly by its military and intelligence agencies. There is little doubt about the government's early and enthusiastic support for the converging systems that make up the Next Internet. It embraced Cloud Computing from the start, ordering government agencies to move to the Cloud before most of those responsible for implementing it understood what the Cloud meant. It did so partly to cut back on its information technology budget. In 2016 the federal government spent about $89 billion on IT with $38 billion going to defense and $51 billion to civilian agencies. This does not include state and local government spending, nor does it include the National Security Agency whose budget remains a secret to all but a select group of government officials. More than cost cutting, the government's embrace is indicative of its enthusiasm to disseminate the use of these systems throughout society. While this is understandable from an economic and social development perspective, there is also a worrisome lack of concern for some of the less than positive social consequences, including expanding surveillance, environmental damage, and the loss of jobs. Nowhere is government enthusiasm made more explicit than in the Obama Administration's 2016 initiative in support of Big Data Analytics, which brought together civilian and military representatives under the management of the National Science Foundation. From its report: "Big Data has the potential to radically improve the lives of all Americans. It is now possible to combine disparate, dynamic, and distributed datasets and enable everything from predicting the future behaviour of complex systems to precise medical treatments, smart energy usage, and focused educational curricula. Government agency research and public-private partnerships, together with the education and training of future data scientists, will enable applications that directly benefit society and the economy of the Nation."[4] Aside from a brief section on ethics, unbridled enthusiasm would not be too extreme a summary of the government's view.

The same enthusiasm has been displayed for the Internet of Things. In January 2017, as the Obama presidency neared its end, the Department of Commerce issued a report called "Fostering the Advancement of the Internet of Things." Once again, notwithstanding some concern about privacy and cybersecurity, the support is clear: "The prospective benefits of IoT to personal convenience, public safety, efficiency, and the environment are clear. IoT has the potential to make our highways safer by enabling connected vehicles to interact with each other to prevent accidents, to make quality health care more accessible through remote monitoring devices and telehealth practices for those who cannot easily travel, and to reduce waste and improve efficiency both in factory supply chains and in the running of cities. It even has the potential to create new industries and consumer goods that have yet to be imagined."[5] Could the enthusiasm be any more unbridled for what some are calling the Internet of Hackable Things?

A critical reason for the government's support, one barely mentioned in official reports like these, is the reliance on Next Internet systems to expand American military power for new weapons systems that can be deployed by U.S. forces and sold to governments around the world. For the armed forces and intelligence agencies, the Cloud, Big Data, and the Internet of Things are essential to meet their massive surveillance requirements, and to build, manage and control weaponized drones and the rest of the increasingly automated system that the United States uses to project force throughout the world. The latter is likely to soon include Lethal Autonomous Weapons Systems better known as killer robots, once used in Iraq to clear explosive devices. The prospect of fighting distant wars without masses of human soldiers makes the growth of military robotics almost certain. Moreover, as one report put it, "They don't get scared. They don't get mad. They don't respond to a situation with rage — and we've seen some tragic consequences of that happening in Iraq and elsewhere where ... a very human soldier reacts to a terrible situation and ends up killing a lot of civilians."[6]

It would not be an exaggeration to conclude that the twin pillars of Next Internet power for the United States are commercial success, led by the Big Five, and military strength, concentrated at the Department of Defense, the National Security Agency, and the Central Intelligence Agency. Together they form what might best be called the "military information complex," successor to the "military industrial complex" that was central to debates about the global political economy from the 1950s on.

The overall power of the American post-Internet corporate and government establishment faces only one major challenge to its hegemony and this comes from China. The United Kingdom and European companies once offered significant competition, particularly in telecommunications, but that is no longer the case. Moreover, Brexit and the rise of right-wing nationalism make it unlikely that the EU can mount a significant response. That is unfortunate for several reasons, not the least of which is the EU's ability to rein in some of the Big Five's excesses. Its role in privacy protection and that of its unions in preserving quality work are among the important contributions that may be lost if the EU's power is further eroded. EU protections against unwarranted surveillance are the strongest in the developed world. Moreover, it was a German union that led the first strike against Amazon, which sought to bring its low-wage, precarious labor model to warehouses in the country. Moreover, European countries have led a retreat from advertising on Google and Facebook owing to the placement of these ads near sites that promote propaganda, fake news, and hate-infused content. UK brands, such as HSBC, Lloyds Bank, the Royal Bank of Scotland, Vodafone, Sky, and Barclays pulled advertising and issued complaints. The UK unit of the big advertising holding company Havas announced that it was suspending all ads posted on Google for its UK clients, including the mobile firm O2 and Domino's Pizza. Havas did so because it feared that Google did not provide a safe environment for its clients, nor one that is regulated sufficiently to meet its brand objectives. This had an influence on U.S. brands, which, soon thereafter, removed advertising associated with racist content on the Google and Facebook platforms. In 2017 the EU launched the largest single attack on a Big Five company by fining Google $2.7 billion for abusing its monopoly by placing its own comparison-shopping site ahead of others in search results. This not only brought business to the company, but it also cost shoppers more because it demoted sites that were actually more popular and provided consumers with a better service. Although the fine and potential precedent represent a substantial issue for Google, it will do nothing to challenge the company's dominance in Europe because there are no EU-based search alternatives.

Absent challenges from United Kingdom and European companies, the only substantial threat comes from China where, with considerable government backing, a handful of corporate giants are beginning to demonstrate some of the power that the dominant American firms exercise throughout the world. The key difference is that the challenge from China does not include the serious attention that EU regulators have paid to issues like concentrated ownership and the loss of privacy.

THE CHALLENGE FROM CHINA

Resembling its larger counterpart Amazon, Alibaba leads the field of competitors from China. An e-commerce giant with control over 40 percent of China's cloud computing industry, Alibaba has built a genuinely global powerhouse. Founded in 1999, it was valued at $260 billion in 2017, roughly that of General Electric, but below any of the Big Five. Although its business remains concentrated in China, Alibaba is increasingly international, selling from warehouses in China and abroad, including four in the United States located on both coasts. By 2017, it did business in 190 countries. Alibaba sells just about everything. In fact, in addition to sales of conventional goods, the company has benefited financially if not in its image, from illegal and counterfeit goods sold through its subsidiary Taobao, described as a free-for-all shopping platform. It also operates a financial services division with a well-regarded payment system and a cloud computing subsidiary, Alibaba Cloud or AliCloud. Like AWS, it started by servicing the company's needs but grew to become a big player in the business of selling storage and services to other institutions. Also like Amazon, Alibaba has ventured into the newspaper business with its purchase of Hong Kong's South China Morning Post, which raised eyebrows because Alibaba's founder Jack Ma has close ties to the Chinese government. Critics feared that, among other concerns, the purchase might damage what remains of Hong Kong's independent voice.

The company has major plans to deepen its global profile, signaling this when it set up a headquarters and a cloud data center in Silicon Valley. Initially built to assist Chinese companies operating in the United States, now it provides services widely and so successfully that it has built a second in the Valley. Along with data centers in Europe, India, and southeast Asia, the company has become a key player in data analytics. Experts remain uncertain about whether it can compete with the U.S. giants in the American marketplace, but they do forecast enough growth to make its AliCloud subsidiary a $9 billion business by 2020. Alibaba is the leading force in the government of China's goal of building a strong global presence in the Next Internet, what it calls its "Internet+" strategy. Business success has strengthened the company's government ties and this worries some in the West for more than just technological and economic reasons. There is also concern about storing and processing increasing amounts of individual and institutional data about Americans and others in data centers controlled by China's cloud companies and accessible to the government of China.

If Alibaba follows along the path of Amazon, then Baidu is China's Google, the dominant search engine in China. Followers of Google would not be surprised to learn that Baidu's products include the world's first and largest Chinese-language query-based searchable online community platform, the world's largest Chinese-language interactive knowledge-sharing platform, and Baidu Encyclopedia, the world's largest user-generated Chinese-language encyclopedia, similar to the Wikipedia. Its search platform includes Maps, Image Search, Video Search, and News Search. Among China's 730 million Internet users, the company enjoys a market share of slightly over 80 percent when measured by advertising revenues and no other company reaches double digits. Like many other firms, Baidu is taking a big leap to the Cloud in part so that it can use stored data to build user profiles that will serve the marketing needs of its client companies and the surveillance demands of the Chinese government.

Access to both Google and Facebook are sharply restricted in China, as are other platforms and news sites like that of the New York Times. This certainly benefits Baidu, but it

also helps China's version of Facebook, the social media service Tencent, and its WeChat and QQ subsidiaries. Valued at
$278 billion, Tencent is the largest company in Asia and, as
of April 2017, the tenth largest public corporation in the
world. QQ is the leading text messaging service in China
with 900 million monthly users and WeChat's social media
site reaches about 800 million in China and around the
world. QQ has historically been viewed as a low tech, low
cost way for people to connect. This is changing now but it
remains the communication means of choice for China's
working class, which the scholar Jack Qiu has demonstrated
to be an important vehicle for labor organizing and protests,
especially among rural migrants to China's industrial factories. Moreover, Tencent is a leader in China's massive gaming
industry and demonstrated this in 2017 when it announced
plans to construct an entire e-sports town in eastern China
which will come complete with an e-sports theme park, an
e-sports university, a cultural and creative park, an animation
industrial park, a creative neighborhood, a Tencent technology innovation community, and a Tencent cloud data center.
The company emerged as a major international player in
2017 when it purchased a five percent stake in the electric
carmaker Tesla for $1.8 billion, making it one of the largest
shareholders in Elon Musk's company. Moreover, like
Alibaba, Tencent does not intend to limit its market to
China. In 2017 it set up shop in Silicon Valley by building a
data center for its expanding U.S. cloud computing services
even as American companies complain they face growing
restrictions when doing the same in China. Moving north
into Amazon and Microsoft territory, Tencent has set up
an artificial intelligence research facility in Seattle, one step
in the Chinese government's commitment to overtake the
United States as the world leader in the field. So as the

Trump Administration cuts back on AI research, China is surging forward.

In addition to these large Next Internet companies, China's state-owned telecommunications firms China Telecom, China Unicom, and China Mobile, connect the world's largest national user base. China Telecom has been an especially strong participant in Cloud Computing, making it second to Alibaba in the China market. The country's primary telecommunications equipment provider Huawei has expanded internationally, but not without controversy. As it sought to create an international market by opening manufacturing and R&D facilities in the West, the government of the United States charged the company with serving as a conduit for the Chinese government and its military. Canada and Australia followed by joining the United States in banning the company from bidding on government contracts. Not deterred, Huawei sponsored a prestigious World Economic Forum conference on the future of Cloud Computing and then focused intensely on leading all equipment companies in the development of next generation (5G) wireless. With 80,000 employees working only on 5G and a massive campaign to lead the pack in having its technology and patents recognized as the de facto standard, Huawei provides a formidable challenge to U.S. leadership in digital equipment provision.

The power of China's dynamic Next Internet industry has extended to the media business where it has lagged behind the big American firms that are bringing together Silicon Valley and Hollywood in alliances that match Big Tech with movies, television, theme parks, and gaming. The leader here by far is the multinational Wanda Group, which is not well known outside China. It should be. Starting with great success in real estate and finance, the company moved forcefully into the cultural industries and their new media spinoffs. Its

Cultural Industry Group covers four areas: film holdings, including AMC Theatres, the largest movie theater owner in the United States, sports, tourism, including theme parks, and children's entertainment. In a clear attempt to build on its success in media, the company announced in March 2017 that it would join IBM to build a cloud computing subsidiary, Wanda Cloud, for its own businesses and to sell services to others. This is a remarkable development for a company with no experience in the Cloud and in a domestic market already dominated by Alibaba and China Telecom. Nevertheless, by giving IBM the opportunity to enter the China market in a big way, Wanda brings along a major cloud company that will provide it with access to Watson, IBMs Big Data Analytics arm. Yet, worries persist that having grown so quickly, Wanda may be heading for a fall, early evidence of which may be foreshadowed in a mid-2017 decision to sell off some of its holdings to pay down debt.

China's Next Internet companies wield considerable power, if not at the level of their American counterparts. Nevertheless, they benefit from a very strong domestic market. With Internet use at 71 percent of the population and smartphone ownership at 68 percent, China has made enormous progress in developing a strong domestic base. Compare this with its neighbor India with only 21 percent Internet use and 18 percent smartphone ownership. Moreover, China's big firms enjoy enormous government support that protects the domestic market by tightly restricting foreign entry. My annual visits to China mean saying good-bye to Google, Facebook, Twitter, the New York Times, and other sites for the duration. Even Microsoft has been forced to modify its Windows operating system to enable Chinese government monitoring as a condition of its use in the country. A special version of the Microsoft operating system Windows 10, modified for surveillance, is used by Chinese government employees.

China is the only nation to defeat the ride-sharing service Uber, which lost $2 billion over the two years it spent in China. In spite of fully cooperating with Chinese authorities, including using Uber technology to report on the whereabouts of dissidents, Uber was essentially forced to sell its China operation to the government's favorite Didi Chuxing. In return, as it was shown the door, Uber was given a stake in the company.

The market for cloud computing services in China is expected to soon reach $20 billion. As elsewhere, government protects its domestic operators by requiring U.S. firms to partner with local cloud businesses. For example, Amazon, which began cloud operations in China in 2013, partners with Beijing Sinnet Technology Co. Ltd. Similarly, Microsoft has a contract with 21Vianet Group, Inc. to deploy its Cloud. But partnerships come with numerous regulations and controls. Foreign cloud businesses are not allowed to invest directly in the cloud infrastructure. Moreover, domestic operators are not permitted to share network data or personal information with their foreign partners. Before data can proceed to servers outside the country, it has to pass through government gateways. Foreign business must also comply with government censorship rules that are sometimes masked by strict compliance procedures. Apple was required to build a data center in China to store information on the Chinese citizens who use their devices in order to enable easier Chinese government access.

As a result, American companies in China still lag behind China's big cloud companies led by Alibaba and China Telecom. Furthermore, American start-ups that cannot get funding are now turning to Chinese investors. This has raised serious concerns in U.S. military and intelligence circles because the start-ups include firms working on technologies with military applications, such as sensors for ships, rocket engines for spacecraft, and screens for aircraft cockpits.

Chinese investors include state-owned firms and companies with close connections to Chinese government officials.

China's Internet+ program, given significant attention in the country's thirteenth Five Year Plan, is part of a wider project with enormous political economic and geopolitical implications. In order to grasp these, it is useful to start with the 2000-year-old project widely known as the Silk Road. This is the name given to a set of trading routes established to connect China with Central Asia. In return for the silk made exclusively in China, merchants brought cattle, horses, hides, furs, as well as luxury items, such as ivory and jade, to China. Over time, new goods, such as foods not available in China, and new skills, including wine making from grapes, were introduced. The trade route endured wars, changes in governments, chronic crime, and other interruptions to sustain a model for long-distance trade. It is such a significant part of the Chinese historical imaginary that the current Chinese government has named its twenty-first century trade-building project the New Silk Road (also less romantically known as Belt and Road or One Belt One Road). Announced in 2013, this ambitious project combines overland and sea routes to connect 60 nations in Asia and Europe to facilitate trade. These make up 60 percent of the population, 75 percent of the energy resources, and 70 percent of GDP in the world. Myriad joint projects encompass a massive land infrastructure of rail lines, bridges, highways, as well as new and refurbished cargo shipping ports. These make it the largest construction scheme of the twenty-first century. Although the new Silk Road draws from many different countries, there is no doubt that China is leading the project. It leads most joint projects and has taken on some of them by itself, notably purchase of the legendary Greek port of Piraeus, which has become the terminus of the China to Europe maritime Silk Road. The overland portion contains a dizzying array of projects, most remarkably, a freight rail line that travels 7,500 miles from eastern China to London, making stops at key hubs during its 15-day journey. As the project intensifies and brings on new partners, it is likely to shift the balance of international trade power. How much is hard to say. But it is not hard to see just how deeply this project has entered the public imagination in China. There is even a set of children's bedtime stories and videos produced by China's Ministry of Propaganda. These celebrate the new Silk Road as China's gift to the world, not failing to mention that the United States has refused to participate. We do indeed make myths when we make technology. In this case, it is the story of uniting the world through infrastructure, a myth that now serves as cultural infrastructure to support a resurgent nationalism.

Belt and Road is just one, admittedly the largest, of several international infrastructure projects that China is leading. Member nations come from all over the world but do not formally include the United States. Nevertheless, the firm leading the world in the industrial Internet of Things, General Electric, has been heavily involved in projects that compensate for shortcomings in the capacity of China's industrial companies to meet the project's massive needs. In 2016 GE provided $2.3 billion in equipment primarily for the New Silk Road project.

Outside the New Silk Road, in February 2017 passengers rode the first transnational electrified train in Africa, taking a 466-mile trek that now links Djibouti and Ethiopia. The six-year project was funded entirely by Chinese banks and was designed and built primarily by Chinese engineers and workers. China is also constructing a $5 billion high-speed rail line in Indonesia, and a 2,400-mile Pan-Asia Rail Network, that will connect China to Laos, Thailand and Singapore. In addition, China has become the world leader in another significant area of infrastructure, the production and sale of solar panels. It is now home to over two-thirds of global production capacity and buys fully half the world's supply. As one analyst concluded, "It now effectively controls the market."[7] On a recent trip on the Shanghai to Wuhan high-speed train, I could not help but notice that even in the tiniest of villages, home rooftops contained solar panels.

These projects could not be completed without major investments in digital technologies to build and manage them. Yet, they do not quite represent the soft power so often associated with film, television, newspapers, and other forms of cultural activism. Nor do they embody the hard power exemplified in military force, which China has projected in the South China Sea to the consternation of Japan, South Korea, and the United States. Rather, they occupy a middle ground that does not attract enough attention because infrastructure talk is never as interesting as debates over movies and bombs. But they are undoubtedly important strategically and are closely tied to China's Internet+ strategy for leadership in the global political economy. This connection has tightened since China instituted its Made in China 2025 program to promote greater self-sufficiency in computer chip manufacturing, electric cars, and other industries that Beijing concluded has led to excessive dependency on the United States. The program is offering low interest loans, research grants, and other government assistance to firms in emerging industries. The goal is to achieve up to 80 percent Chinese ownership of a select group of industries in eight years. Critics charge that this would violate the spirit, if not the letter, of the law enshrined in the World Trade Organization. Whether or not it does, Made in China represents a strong challenge to American domination of the IT and social media sector. Apple is especially worried that this might diminish its relationship with the Foxconn Technology Group, its primary contractor in China, which is based in Taiwan, as the Chinese government promotes local firms like Huawei and Xiaomi.

There are no guarantees that China's infrastructure projects and Made in China policies will meet their goals. Massive government-sponsored construction projects that have worked inside China might get bogged down, if not end in disaster, when infrastructure plans crash into domestic politics (can China's economy sustain this amount of investment?) and international politics (can China actually bring together whole regions of nations in dizzyingly complex projects?). Moreover, American firms are not standing still. In February 2017 Facebook announced that it and two partners would build 500 miles of fiber optic cable in Uganda and add three million more Internet users to Africa's meager total. Nevertheless, Beijing's strong moves in middle and soft power make more clear the Obama Administration's push to create and promote aggressively the Trans-Pacific Partnership trade pact that was to have expanded liberalized trade with a group of Asian nations, as well as with Australia, New Zealand, Chile, Peru, Mexico, and Canada. China was excluded primarily because the United States wanted to slow down its major competitor's push for leadership of the global political economy and to demonstrate that the United States remained able to play a dominant role in international trade. Of course, all this was dashed with the Trump victory. The TPP was never very popular politically. There were fears that it would cost jobs and would also tighten restrictions on intellectual property, making medicines less accessible. The irony of Trump's decision to pull out of the agreement was that it handed a victory to China, a nation he vilified throughout his campaign. Sure enough, China has stepped into the void by joining a meeting of the original TPP participants, minus the United States and including South Korea, to discuss the possibility of what was called a regional trade pact, but was actually, in effect, an attempt to forge a new TPP deal with China replacing the United States. Moreover, China has directly challenged U.S. leadership in global development assistance by leading the formation of the Asian Infrastructure Investment Bank. With member nations from everywhere in the world, with the notable exception of the United States, the Bank provides an alternative to the International Monetary Fund, which the United States has led since its founding in 1945.

The Next Internet is intimately connected to the global political economy and the intensifying geopolitical tensions between the United States and China. From a chapter that addressed the digital body politic, we next take up the digital political body.

CHAPTER 4

THE BODY AND CULTURE

What the market now seems to require is an imagined future exotic enough to be thrilling but recognizable enough to be credible.

— Steven Shapin

SKIN IN THE GAME

In 2017, MIT's Media Lab, the Vatican of digital technology experimentation, innovation, and development, introduced DuoSkin. Created in partnership with Microsoft Research, it takes temporary tattoos and turns them into connected interfaces enabling them to serve as input for smartphones, tablets, and computers. They can also display in different colors based on changes in body temperature and transmit data to other devices. In a short video on the tattoos, a developer talks about the marriage of aesthetics and functionality: "I think there is no better fashion statement than to change how your skin looks."[8] The designs, which include abstract geometrics, flowers, and hearts, feature gold leaf, which is pictured sprinkled on chocolate candy or floating in a vodka drink. But the pleasures of this fashion statement are special. First, they can be used as an input controller enabling the wearer to, for example, adjust a music player. Next, they provide output displays that enable the tattoo to change colors based on changes in body temperature or even light up to show a current emotional state. Finally, the tattoos serve as communication devices, such as NFC tags, that allow users to read data directly from skin. The developers promote them as expanding personal freedom because they make it possible to change a personal aesthetic and appearance instantly. Moreover, because they are inexpensive to produce, DuoSkins can be made widely accessible so that practically anyone can enjoy their upscale look and functionality. They offer a simple and inexpensive way to make a fashion statement and to expand one's digital world. The body beautiful meets the body digital.

GETTING CHIPPED

Let us leave the Media Lab for a trip to Stockholm and the Epicenter, a tech hub, which has begun another experiment in body enhancement, the insertion of digital devices the size of a grain of rice under the skin. These mini chips, similar to those stored in transit passes, transmit personal security information over short distances to specially equipped receivers. Stored in a card, they allow the user to enter a transit platform. Stored under the skin, they permit workers to enter secure areas and enable them to use digital devices like workspace computers without having to enter passwords. They also deliver valuable information to the company, including an opportunity to constantly track the chipped employee's location. The devices are put in place with a syringe, which slides into the flesh between the thumb and the index finger. One click later and the microchip is injected into the hand.

The primary justification is convenience. As the person responsible for implanting the chips noted, "Today it's a bit messy — we need pin codes and passwords — wouldn't it be easy to just touch with your hand?"[9] This is not the first human chip implant, but arguably the first on such a large scale. The company responsible for them is the bio-hacking firm BioNyfiken, which is using Epicenter as a test case to explore what happens when a large number of employees are chipped. By the spring of 2017, 150 Epicenter workers had the implants. Expecting a less than positive response to the news, the person heading the project gives it a positive spin: "We want to be able to understand this technology before big corporates and big government come to us and say everyone should get chipped — the tax authority chip, the Google or Facebook chip."[10] In July 2017, a tech company in Wisconsin announced a similar plan with 50 of its 80 employees already chipped and a company in Belgium has offered its workers the same chip implant option. These will not be the last.

I decided to start this chapter on digital technologies, bodies, and culture with these two examples because they share important perspectives on the quantified self. First, each assumes that wearing chips on or under the skin is inevitable. There is no turning back, so acceptance on our terms is preferable to rejection. Second, in their own ways, each proposes ways to cope, with one demonstrating how to aestheticize the inevitable by turning devices into fashion statements and the other viewing experiments on chipped people as opportunities to determine how to use them wisely. Finally, they each embody elements of myths that the chapter explores. These include the myth of the singularity or the belief that people are slowly merging with machines and that it is our fate to take the next evolutionary leap and create a genuine trans-humanism. The fashionable but connected tattoo and the chip on the equivalent of a grain of rice take small steps toward this ultimate goal. They also advance a second myth that is foundational for the Next Internet. Next Internet systems, especially the Internet of Things, are more than banal instruments to meet economic or political goals. They are also cultural objects that signify a range of meanings. Like tribal totems, they have magical qualities that embody the sublime. In this case, it is the belief that inert, inorganic things can come alive, register emotions in the case of the tattoo, open secure locks and login to computers in the case of the chip implant. They take admittedly tiny steps to ground these mythic beliefs but they also participate in a technological complex that contains profound political economic and cultural power.

COUNT AND COMMODIFY

There is nothing particularly new about quantifying the individual. We have been counting people, their activities, and their internal processes for many years. The field of Population Studies or what is now called the discipline of Demography has been with us since ancient Greece. Tax authorities have kept track of income for even longer, dating back to the Egyptian Pharaohs and their tax collecting scribes. Taking readings of body functions originated with the Babylonians. What is new is the seemingly unlimited capacity to quantify, store, process, and use the results of the data these measurements generate.

There is also nothing especially new about inserting measurement devices inside the body. Pacemakers to keep the heart working properly have been around since 1958, long before the Internet appeared. What is new is the capacity to apply digital technology to measure and monitor more, if not most, of what the body is doing. These readings come from devices, like our digital grain of rice, that are inserted into the body or from drug-dispensing devices that are similarly inserted for those who cannot, or do not want to, ingest pills and medicines. They are also taken from devices placed on or near the body such as the temporary tattoo, or more likely the smartphone in the pocket that counts steps, or the watch on the wrist that can provide a heart rate reading. Measurements also come from the many monitoring devices, from street cameras to computerized tollbooths that measure our activities as a routine part of daily life. As the satellite tracking devices that keep a close eye on truck drivers or send weaponized drones to their targets demonstrate, these do not even have to be near people to measure, monitor, quantify, and communicate their activities.

Opportunities to quantify the self are now practically everywhere and with the Cloud we have enormously expanded the capacity to store the information they gather. Moreover, Big Data Analytics has vastly enlarged the ability to process, analyze, and turn these data into predictive algorithms. Finally, the Internet of Things makes it possible to send out readings on our bodies, their activities and internal processes into the constantly flowing and interconnected streams of local and global networks. As a result, it has become popular to refer to the *quantified* self as a fact of life in the post-Internet world. The term is sometimes used to simply capture the growing tendency to focus on quantitative readings of bodily activities. It is also used, however, in the critical sense of reducing the self to a quantity by turning personal identity into nothing more than a statistical reading, at the expense of the qualitative, subjective, and otherwise unquantifiable dimensions of life. The poet Lord Byron would agree: "The tree of knowledge," he insisted, "is not the tree of life." To that I would simply add: nor does a forest of data make a living society.

While continuing to use the term quantified self, it is arguably just as important, if not more useful, to refer to the *commodified* self, an increasingly key component in a social process of turning people, places, and things into marketable products. Specifically, commodification is the process of taking goods and services which are valued for their use, for example, food to satisfy hunger, stories we tell our friends, and transforming them into commodities which are valued for what they can earn in the marketplace, for example, farming to sell food or producing entertainment stories for video outlets. The process of commodification is doubly important for understanding the digital world. First, digital technologies and practices contribute to the general commodification process throughout society. For example, the introduction of computers gave businesses more control over the entire process of production, distribution, and exchange, permitting firms to monitor sales and inventory levels with ever-improving precision. Second, commodification is a key to understand specific digital industry institutions and practices. For example, the worldwide expansion of commodification in the 1980s, responding in part to global declines in economic growth, led to the increased commercialization of news, the privatization of once public media and telecommunications institutions, and the liberalization of communication markets. It contributed to diminishing the public interest component of these organizations and accentuated their more profitable entertainment dimensions.

Commodification is now at work on the self in the post-Internet world. Much is owed to the technology-enabled surveillance projects of U.S. intelligence agencies that began at the end of World War II with major strides made by the

National Reconnaissance Office, an agency founded in 1961 but whose existence was not acknowledged for 30 years, and the now well-known National Security Agency. Starting with photographs from weather balloons, these surveillance agencies moved on to communication satellites. The NSA pioneered the development of electronic voice surveillance in the 1970s and 1980s, capturing the content of telephone calls worldwide and processing them through word filters that enabled the Agency to store sensitive communication for later action.

Building on these early surveillance efforts, today's digital companies use Internet-enabled devices to monitor individuals, capture data, store it in cloud computing data centers and process it with Big Data Analytics. For example, when Amazon's digital assistant Alexa or Apple's Siri is given a voice command, such as "Siri, play the song 'We the People' by A Tribe Called Quest," the device not only activates an audio player to meet the request, it also sends the requested information to a data center for processing. At some point, this information flows through a stream of similar data that is marketed to companies interested in advertising to the person who made the request, as well as to the person's online friends, and others who share characteristics, beliefs, and interests with that person. The use value contained in the request for a song is turned into exchange value when a company pays for the knowledge of the music that interests the user. Similarly, when one walks down the street with an iPhone in the hand, a Fitbit in the pocket, or an Apple Watch on the wrist, the device counts precisely how many steps you have walked. This certainly contributes to the quantified self, but it also enables the marketing of that information to companies that use the data to sharpen the ability to customize advertising, thereby contributing to the commodified self. That same device, or one of dozens of others, provides information on a user's body functions that is useful to assess overall health before, during, and after exercise. However, it is also valued by advertisers who will pay for the data to customize the user's ad space and by risk assessment firms interested in using the data to make a medical insurance assessment. Credit bureaus also want the data to determine if a customer can borrow to buy a home, as well as to establish the particular rate category that fits one's data profile. In all these cases, a distinct part of the user's self is commodified, turned into a product to be marketed and sold.

As scholars put it, the commodified self is organized into a *panoptic sort*. First, ubiquitous surveillance gathers as much data as possible, creating a digital version of the all-seeing Panopticon that the philosopher Jeremy Bentham envisioned. Next these data on the self are sorted into the categories that customized marketing and risk assessment institutions require. With information on an individual's financial transactions, a company assigns a credit score, one of the major marks of the commodified self. It is no huge leap to conclude that before too long, the score becomes an integral part of one's self-definition, representing more than just an indicator of creditworthiness.

We are only in the early stages of developing the digital devices that contribute to commodifying the self. Yet, they seem to be, or soon will be, everywhere, measuring and monitoring nearly all aspects of human physical and mental functioning. Each of the top five Next Internet companies is involved in a big way. So too are many others. There are toys that not only entertain children, they also record voices in the living room and transmit them for packaging as a marketable product. The FBI considers this such a serious issue that in July 2017 it issued a public service announcement warning parents that sensor-equipped toys posed the danger of identity theft and child exploitation. "Smart" televisions pose a similar threat. So too do thermostats that decide if you need more heat and refrigerators that tell when the family needs milk. Like the Internet of Things tattoo that began this chapter, these devices are sold as life enhancers, teaching us how to better ourselves, improving our physical and mental health, through quantification. However, just how much they enhance life is questionable, particularly in light of how constant, if not obsessive, attention to the quantities of life can diminish attention to its qualities or, even worse, can reduce these qualities to a set of data points. Commercial surveillance is often defended on the grounds that users are generally given opportunities to opt out of sharing data. However, the ability to prevent sharing is often embedded in agreements that are too difficult to navigate and understand, even for experienced users. Not all companies sell data, choosing to concentrate on the devices alone. However, once they recognize that even a Teddy Bear can transmit marketable data, they often change their approach.

We have come a long way from the time when Google innocently and earnestly pronounced that it would never include advertising on its search site because doing so would bias the results. Today, Google commodifies search requests and those doing the searching by selling information on what is sought to advertisers whose pitches appear in subsequent searches and in those online sites users happen to visit. Google was right. Advertising does bias search results. But the earnings from ads also made it tempting enough for Google to retire its moral compass. Facebook does the same, commodifying the thoughts, ideas, opinions, emotional states, and images of its two billion users. Microsoft makes use of data stored in its Azure cloud computing service to add to its bottom line. Customers, who once relied on discs and CDs to provide essential software and their own hard drives for storage, now increasingly head to the Microsoft Cloud. Amazon commodifies the data generated by all of the devices it sells. There is value in the things that are digitized and connected in the Internet of Things, but there is often more to be made from the data the devices generate, the valuable information that makes up the commodified self. This helps to explain why so many of these tech firms are now engaged in a pitched battle with banks and other financial institutions over who gets to control and sell data on their customers. Tech companies want access to these data to build valuable products, for example, by combining credit card details with mortgage information. In response to the banks' claim that they want to restrict access to protect customer privacy, tech companies accuse finance companies of caring more about their business models and the competitive threat posed by disruptive technologies. The commodified self is a contested terrain in business battles that are only just beginning.

THE WORKER COMMODITY

It is not only the consumer self that is quantified and commodified; the working self is similarly turned into a marketable product and a data point to be controlled. In fact, it is arguably the case that much of what we term consumption is looking more like labor as the concept of delivering audiences to advertisers spreads from old media to the Internet and then on to the post-Internet world. Back in the heyday of broadcast and cable television, programmers would boast about delivering more people of a certain demographic slice to advertisers. It might be young people; it might be women; it might be top spenders. The point was that in an era when value was measured in cost per thousand, the lingo for the most effective audience purchase, it was reasonable to begin thinking about audiences as laborers who, however voluntarily and even gleefully, permitted their attention to be sold to advertisers. This process was refined in the Internet era as companies gathered ever more detailed information on users thereby enabling advertisers to target with greater specificity than broadcasting could ever achieve. With access to users' email, search requests, and social media posts, companies like Google and Facebook were better able to deliver people with very specific tastes, for example, young men who like to trick out Hondas, older women who golf three times a week with expensive clubs, or young women who are likely to be pregnant.

When users provide information to Internet Service Providers like AT&T, platform companies like Google and Facebook, they can be seen to be working because they add value to the site they are using. They may or may not be performing labor in the strict sense of the word, but their activity enables a very successful business process. One need look no further than the book value of companies that produce no tangible product (Facebook), almost none (Google sells a smartphone), or who, like Apple, Microsoft, and Amazon, make some things but earn important portions of their revenue from the value of their customer base. Beyond the Big Five, there is Snap, parent of the popular image site Snapchat, valued at about $30 billion, Twitter worth $11 billion, and Instagram, which, if it were not part of Facebook is estimated to be worth in the vicinity of $33 billion. The value of these companies is almost entirely based on the work of users whose emails, searches, and posts are turned into marketable commodities. In return, users receive no wage, save for the opportunity to continue to access these sites. The Next Internet, with its ubiquitous monitoring and data gathering, deepens and extends the process of commodifying the user-worker.

Attention, clicks, searches, and posts create one kind of worker. Another type is the person who is more actively engaged in the digital world, in areas like fan culture, gaming, and free software. Increasingly it is referred to as *playbour*, an admittedly awkward term, to describe the convergence of playful and hobbyist activities with work. Those who restrict their social media activities to liking a fan site or clicking for more information on a current star increase the value of a site by allowing information about them to be commodified. Those engaged in playbour go beyond this by joining a fan group that actively promotes a star, publicizing and building enthusiasm for the star's work. They might also suggest valuable ways to improve the site, bring in new fans, and generate new publicity. Unpaid for their work, they nevertheless generate value for the star, the star's business, and the social media sites they use.

Gamers get together to improve the latest product, debug beta versions of games, and promote their favorites online. In the extreme, game enthusiasts also known as gold farmers spend long hours on massively multiplayer online games to earn virtual currencies that they can trade for real world money. Rich players who do not want to spend time actually playing the games, hire gold farmers who play for them. Estimates run to over a million gold farmers in China alone mostly toiling in the electronic sweatshops of Internet cafés. Whether just a game enthusiast or a gold farmer, skill and love of the game are turned into labor that benefits game corporations and the entire online apparatus that profits from their hours online.

Back in the 1920s, before radio went from hobby to commercial business, amateur operators set up stations that broadcast from their homes to whoever had a receiver capable of tuning in. Mythologized as the "Radio Boys," they pioneered the technology they loved for no financial reward.

Tall tales were written about their heroics but there is no denying the positive impact they had in developing broadcast technology and promoting the use of radio. Commercial radio took advantage of their contribution just as today's new media companies benefit from amateur fan groups and gamers. The computer era has its own version of the amateur radio boys. These are the information technology enthusiasts who write programs, debug software, hack weak systems, and otherwise live for the world of code. Many of them fit the model of playbour. They may have a day job that has nothing to do with computing, but the work they love to play at is software. Uncompensated, they play a vital role in promoting information technology and the industry that profits from their devotion. Their labor is often commodified but they retain a sense of play and of working for themselves and not just for a wage.

The commodification of the worker self is made complete in the world of wage labor. When thoughts turn to employment in the tech industry, especially for the top companies, they are filled with visions of opulent workplaces with plenty of games, good food, freedom, and a casual atmosphere. Google, which sits atop *Fortune* magazine's list of the top 100 companies in the United State to work for, has become the model for this dream. The company is well known for its luxury extras like free chef-prepared food, laundry, and personal grooming services. It set the industry standard for parental leave, supports transgender rights, holds serious workshops on race and gender bias, and generally promotes an inclusive and safe workplace. Engineers design their own workspaces, choose their preferred ergonomic furniture, and use just the right workout equipment. As long as they satisfy the requirements of their work group, they can come and go as they please. Given all the perks, most remain.

Not all companies, not even other elite Next Internet firms, are as generous as Google. Nevertheless, most share in what is rightly called the "tech aristocracy," whose commodified work selves are richly rewarded. However, this is only a thin sliver of the labor force in these industries. The previous chapter described much less privileged stops on the global computer supply chain, including those who extract rare metals in dangerous African mines and hardware assemblers in Asia who work long hours in workplaces filled with hazardous chemicals. There are also the commercial content moderators, workers whose job it is to scrub social media sites, mobile apps, and cloud services of highly offensive, often violent and sexual content, before it reaches users. This is not the hateful bigotry that has led advertisers to flee Google and YouTube. It is far worse. These employees protect users by sifting through this verbal trash and identifying posts that are so offensive they must be rejected before appearing on social media sites. Most commercial content moderators work in Asia, primarily the Philippines, for low wages, $100 per week is typical, filling their day with long hours spent staring into an ugly sea of depravity. Things got so bad for content moderators at Microsoft that they sued the company, claiming that exposure to images of "indescribable sexual assaults" and "horrible brutality" led to severe post-traumatic stress disorder (PTSD). Microsoft did nothing but dispute the claims. This also appears to be the case at Facebook where, according to Sarah T. Roberts, a leading academic expert in the field, "People can be highly affected and desensitized. It's not clear that Facebook is even aware of the long term outcomes, never mind tracking the mental health of the workers."[11] As a result, many leave after a short time because the work is difficult to bear. Their laboring selves are not only commodified, they are thoroughly degraded. Nevertheless, at 100,000, the number of content moderators totals twice those working for Google and 14 times the Facebook workforce.

In the West, there is a growing category known as "gig" workers for their labor in an industry that produces a steady stream of gigabyte data. It is so large that those toiling in the "gig economy" have become iconic for the fate of employment in the Next Internet era. Not easy to define, even the U.S. Bureau of Labor Statistics, whose job it is to do just that, has a hard time describing the gig economy. Suffice it to say that it is an industry with many one-off or on-demand jobs, where workers are hired in a digital marketplace mainly for companies with a strong tech presence. Common characteristics now include low-wages, precarious work, and no benefits other than a wage that might be based on a specific task or time worked. One estimate concludes that 4 million Americans now work in the gig economy and the number is expected to surpass 9 million by 2021. Amazon is a leader in the field with its Mechanical Turks, workers who are hired on a piece work basis carrying out one job at a time, usually involving tasks that computers alone cannot carry out. A company or person who might need someone to find objects in photographs, write comments for a website or participate in a social science experiment, will post the job on Amazon's site and set a payment price. These Requesters then choose among the applicants who are called Providers or Turkers. With low piece-rate payments and little protection for Turkers, exploitation has been rampant and some have banded together to organize online. Nevertheless, given the number of people who need extra cash or who want the freedom to work only on short-term projects, the service remains popular. With Mechanical Turk, Amazon built the foundation for jobs that require little investment in workers who use their own tools to complete a task, are paid little, and receive no company perks, certainly a far cry from playing foosball at Google's headquarters.

The icon for gig economy labor is the ride-sharing firm Uber, which has combined technological prowess with precarious labor to shakeup the taxi industry in much of the world. Using digital technology to match drivers with riders and to measure, monitor, and quantify, with the help of riders, the precise value of driver labor, Uber has become a $60 billion company. But there is a big price to be paid for disruption and much of it boils down to treating managers and drivers as fully commodified selves whose total dedication is expected. The company employs hundreds of social scientists and data specialists to manage and manipulate the behavior of drivers to obtain the maximum amount of work for the lowest possible wage with the least disruption and resistance. Given its ability to measure and monitor the precise details of driver behavior, such as breaking and acceleration speed, and the precise details of traffic flows, Uber management can exercise extraordinary control over its workforce.

Nowhere is the fully commodified worker better captured than in a 2016 incident involving Uber's main U.S. competitor Lyft, which portrays itself as the more warm-hearted of the two industry disrupters. That image took a revealing turn when its public relations department decided to publicize the remarkable dedication of one of its drivers who, although nine-months pregnant and experiencing the onset of labor contractions, kept picking up fares. Thankfully, her final ride request was a short one that, as the contractions deepened, gave her barely enough time to give birth without incident. To Lyft, the driver is a worker hero, so devoted to her job that she worked until the baby arrived. The driver is celebrated in a post, complete with a photo of her new daughter pictured wearing a "Little Miss Lyft" onesie, as if to announce that the company was not only slapping its brand on her mom. The post concludes by calling on Lyft workers to share similar "exciting Lyft stories." This is not the reluctant acceptance of the fully quantified and commodified worker in a world of constant disruption. It is a call to celebrate those courageous enough to give up their bodies fully and completely to the company. Lyft did not offer to raise her pay, which is abysmally low, especially considering that drivers use their own automobiles. The company did not offer to provide her with health insurance, maternity leave, or any benefits at all. Companies like Uber and Lyft view these as drags on the digital gig economy. Perhaps, these are the reasons why she drove to the end of her pregnancy. She had to. In a play on the standard view that gig economy workers do it for the freedom, a *Gizmodo* story commented: "Maybe she's an heiress who happens to love the freedom of chauffeuring strangers from place to place on her own schedule. But that Lyft, for some reason, thought that this would reflect kindly on them is perhaps the most horrifying part."[12]

It may be horrifying, but there is nothing exceptional in Lyft's response. Consider the company Fiverr, which has raised over \$110 million in venture capital funds to support a business that matches buyers and sellers of digital services, including people who charge as little as \$5, hence the name, to carry out a service like making a creative happy birthday video. Fiverr not only celebrates quantified and commodified workers, but it also delivers its vision with a slick aesthetic. "In Doers We Trust" is an advertising campaign that, in stark black, white and gray images, profiles people who give up everything, endure every hardship, to succeed as "doers." Insisting in its ads that these are not thinkers, dreamers, or planners, Fiverr just wants doers. As one puts it: "You eat your coffee for lunch. You follow through on your follow through. Sleep deprivation is your drug of choice. You might be a doer."[13] The company that identifies itself as the world's largest marketplace for digital services presents its icon of the gig economy as someone who gives up food and sleep to work as a low wage freelancer. Moreover, even with that degree of what is best described as self-abuse, in the eyes of the company, the enterprising young woman might, or perhaps might not, qualify as a doer. In essence, there is nothing one can do to guarantee an escape from the inherent precariousness of the digital world. As a consumer or worker, there is no easy way to flee the quantified and commodified self.

CHILD'S PLAY

Nor does it help to be a child. That is because the model of how a computer operates or "thinks" is now a staple for teaching pre-school and school-age youngsters. The buzzword is computational learning and although it is most popular in university courses, enthusiasts are encouraging parents to insist that childcare centers and elementary schools make it available to their children. It is responsible for the revival of computer science departments, whose very survival was threatened when the IT bubble burst at the turn of the century and were once again threatened by the financial meltdown of 2008. Computer science classrooms are now full to capacity and departments are turning away potential majors. Philosophy departments teach the same things, often with great skill and depth, but computer science has the added benefit of sprinkling a little Silicon Valley gold dust on those who learn its principles and practices.

Gold dust aside, there is nothing especially novel about computational learning. It brings together logical and analytical ways of thinking that were once mainstays of curricula, but which have since been discarded for more "practical"

approaches. The best of computational learning is the legitimacy it offers to tried and true methods for "how to think"
such as generalizing from a handful of observations.
Unfortunately, it also involves attempts to teach the details of
computer coding that are best left to specialized courses. If
the image of preschoolers given a batch of old-fashioned
blocks to learn the rudiments of programming seems to be
more than a bit over the top, it is. What makes computational learning more significant, and more insidious, is the
widely accepted view that computers hold the key to thinking
and learning. It is not enough to teach computers how to
think like humans. With computational learning, the goal is
to teach humans to think like computers. Along with the
quantified and commodified self, the computerized brain
challenges what it means to be a human being.

METAPHORICALLY SPEAKING

It is not unusual to draw on the metaphors dominant in one
sphere of life to describe and explain all of life. Changes in
metaphors signal changes in the underlying culture. Once it
was religion. Raised a Roman Catholic, I was taught to think
about the world as the "mystical body of Christ" because the
Son of God contained the multitude of living things. Nature
has also given us the language we still use to explain the
world. These include metaphors of growth and decay, of
sowing seeds of rebellion and then nipping them in the bud.
However, from the seventeenth century on, the language of
technology increasingly came to fill narrative space once
occupied by religion and by nature. No longer an extension
of divine will, the universe after Isaac Newton took on the
form of a well-built clock, given its initial wind-up in a divine
workshop, but from then on just ticking away on its own. It

should therefore come as no surprise that with the rise of computers, we would begin to see society as a self-regulating cybernetic mechanism, institutions and organizations as software programs, and the building blocks of life as pieces of code. As one expert muses on how we think today, "There is a tendency to rephrase every assertion about mind or brains in computational terms."[14]

As the Next Internet dawns, it is increasingly common to draw from the metaphor of the software stack. In strict technological terms, a stack refers to a collection of different pieces of software that are brought together to accomplish a task. Cloud experts refer to the software stack that runs a data center. Big Data Analytics specialists speak about the correct stack data structure. Those developing Internet of Things devices refer to the application stack. The stack might include software to run hardware, an operating system to manage programs, and application software to connect the user to specific content. An effective stack has all of these working together smoothly. So far, so good. But like many technical terms, meaning begins to leak outside the world that gave it life. Facebook is a social media stack whose pieces fit well together. Twitter's do not. Digital assistants are said to have different personality stacks. Beyond the tech world, nutrition enthusiasts now discuss their supplement stack and entertainment critics refer to a talent stack.

Inevitably, we now have the stacked self, with the "right" personality comprised of the best combination of programs and routines that fit best in the contemporary social stack. Such talk can be easily dismissed as the meaningless and harmless buzzword-filled chatter that results from too much attention to screens. At best, it can be aspirational, the language that helps people figure out what is wrong in their lives and make adjustments. Code is not inscribed in stone. Software can be rewritten; life can be hacked. But at worst, the language can be confining, if not imprisoning because it locks us into one world of thought, a world that is increasingly built on the foundation of quantification and commodification. In this case, the self becomes a stack of data points whose parameters are set by those driven to commercialize just about everything.

MYTH-ING LINKS

Left in the hands of Big Tech, ours is increasingly a world where daily life, as consumers and as workers, is increasingly quantified and commodified. The tendency is both voluntary and forced. We see the opportunity for greater convenience and possible self-improvement in choosing to have Alexa turn on the house lights, by asking Siri to deliver a favorite playlist, and deciding to wear footstep counters that it is hoped will deliver improved physical fitness. Many have no problem with Amazon's Echo Show which puts a screen on the home appliance speaker allowing selected friends to do an electronic "pop in," by appearing on the home screen unannounced. Most recognize that the price of such convenience is delivering more and more information to commercial enterprises that use it to advertise to users and their networks. Some of these also know that their data will make their way to risk assessment businesses that use the tools of Big Data Analytics to determine credit worthiness for a car loan, mortgage, or private medical and life insurance. In these cases it becomes an accepted tradeoff, sort of voluntary and sort of forced.

For many, if not most, caught up in the great panoptic sort, the voluntary aspects are not especially clear. With monopolies and monopsonies on key gateways, the Big Five appear to leave little choice: Google is where we go to search or send email; Microsoft to process words and numbers; Facebook to connect with friends; Amazon to buy things and store our data; and Apple for the phone everyone seems to own. There are alternatives and some choose them but they are more difficult to reach, to navigate, and most of them are also immersed in commodification. The genuine exceptions are public service institutions like schools, libraries, and the postal service, which still operate primarily on universalistic principles and eschew, by law or regulation, commodifying every transaction. But the alternatives are shrinking in most places or taking on the look of private enterprise, and jettisoning consumer protections in defense of efficiency, populism or progress. Another alternative is to simply shun the digital world and its compelling, if not addicting, characteristics and spend more time in nature, in the analog world, and in the rich subjectivity of human relationships. Chapter six considers this worthy alternative by exploring the potential for a less commercial and more democratic post-Internet society. For now it is important to acknowledge what for many is the inescapable need to join a world of wage labor that is awash in jobs that quantify and commodify the self. A job at places like Google is the lottery prize in the world of work. But aside from the challenges that these jobs pose, in complete dedication to the company for an admittedly rich financial reward, they represent a small portion of total employment in the post-Internet world. More are to be found in precarious employment, for piece rates, that come with incessant monitoring that increasingly occupies non-work time and people's emotional lives. People who give up more of their personal lives to work (one more fare and then I'll have that baby, why not have coffee for lunch, sleep is for the slothful) or remake their subjective and emotional selves (the constant smile and feigned pleasantries) are applauded as role models in post-Internet mythology.

The digital world's myth of the "doer" relies on a deeper set of myths that provide it with cultural justification. Fiverr's myth is a story about what it means to be successful. Do not dream or even think, it insists, just act. The test of the myth is not the falsification of the strategy. Even if it could be tested and somehow proven false, the myth would persist if enough people continued to believe that the act comes before everything and that there is nothing more important than giving your life to your job. The myth would disappear if people chose to stop maintaining it, if they decided to cease telling its stories, practice its supporting rituals, and moved on to more sustainable tales. Although they are influenced by, and also help shape, political, economic, and social institutions, myths are deeply cultural because, at root, they are about making meaning through stories and about enacting values in discourse. Most are closely tied to specific social practices, including performances and rituals, both religious and secular. They were once largely about addressing questions that arose in the context of religion. Who or what is god? Later they became more prominent in discourse about the natural world. How to explain the universe? Or the awe inspired by a natural wonder?

For the past 200 years they have been increasingly associated with technology, especially communication technology. This should come as no surprise. The natural wonders that once anchored the sublime are replaced by environmental devastation. Great photographs of the environment are no longer representations of beauty, however stark. Edward Burtynsky's images of the shock and awe that corporate greed inflicts on the land and sea have replaced Ansel Adams' beatific visions of Yosemite National Park. So when it comes to the sublime, we now turn to technology.

It is no exaggeration to suggest that when we make technology, we do not only build machines, but also we build myths. To assert that the telegraph would bring world peace, that the telephone would speed gender equality, that radio would build a world community, and if not radio, then television, was to make a myth of communication technology.

THE SINGULARITY IS NEAR

Today, myths about technology anchor sublime visions contained in the promise of using digital systems to extend life, even achieve immortality, in what mythmakers call the *singularity*, the merging of humans and machines. Inspired especially by the Internet of Things, a second mythology is taking hold and that is the ability to *bring things to life*. They are both key myths of post-Internet society. The concept of the singularity has been around in one form or another since the 1950s when the polymath John van Neumann used the term to describe a process whereby machines equipped with artificial intelligence enter an accelerated learning phase to produce a superintelligence. The computer scientist, inventor, and a director of engineering at Google, Raymond Kurzweil, is most responsible for popularizing the term, gaining notoriety for insisting that if humans take advantage of this development, they can achieve immortality. He has gone as far as setting out a specific timetable of development leading to the human—computer convergence that will end with the singularity in 2045. At that point, tiny, advanced Internet of Things devices, known as nanobots, which will have already spent years working inside human bodies to maintain them in good health, will connect our brains to a version of the computer brain we call today the Cloud. In essence, people will jack into the Next Internet. Eventually, biological bodies will become anachronistic and people will live on, perhaps forever, participating in the collective cloud consciousness. This certainly sounds like the stuff of science fiction and the genre has indeed influenced thinking about the singularity, especially Arthur C. Clarke's classic *Childhood's End*. But proponents are very serious and supporters, including some of Silicon Valley's elite, are investing large sums to help make it happen. These include Kurzweil's employer Google, which in 2013 injected a billion dollars into a secretive anti-aging project, Google Calico, that received the enthusiastic support of the company's founders Sergey Brin and Larry Page. In 2017 the founder and CEO of Tesla and SpaceX, Elon Musk, in spite of his professed fear and public warnings about the dangers of AI, set up a new company called Neuralink that works on brain implants it hopes will someday connect human brains with AI systems. Much of this thinking is based on new developments in syringe-injectible electronics, which suggests that the brain—machinery connection can be made minimally invasive by using wireless technology rather than, for example, a suppurating, infection-prone piercing of the skull. The research arm of the Defense Department, always on the lookout for the latest in cyber-technologies that might produce next generation transhuman warriors, is also investing in the direct brain—machine connection. Concentrating on implantable neural devices, the Pentagon's aim is "to provide unprecedented signal resolution and data-transfer bandwidth between the human brain and the digital world."[15]

Kurzweil's ideas received additional affirmation in 2017 when the best-selling historian Yuval Noah Harari published a book with the less than subtle title *Homo Deus*, a follow up to his magisterial *Sapiens: A Brief History of Humankind*. The former makes the case that within a century technologies will fundamentally transform the human race into god-like creatures powered by artificial intelligence and a host of technologies that emerge from a revolution he calls *dataism*. In essence, humans take an evolutionary leap to become the

Next Internet, the flesh and machine equivalent of highly connected nodes in networks of data and flows of information. Pointing to Kurzweil, Harari worries that this vision can all too easily be turned into a religion of technology. Nevertheless, he fully embraces the vital core that underlies his concerns. When asked if people should resist a future of inevitable technological advancement and create a different futurism, he is quick to reply: "You can't stop technological progress." Moreover, "it's the same with artificial intelligence and bioengineering. So I think people shouldn't be focused on the question of how to stop technological progress because this is impossible."[16]

Whether or not, as Kurzweil insists, "the singularity is near," and whether or not the entire project has scientific warrant, as myth it tells a compelling story: technology, especially digital technology, is powerful, benign, and irresistible. There is no point whatsoever in opposing the Next Internet because the Cloud, Big Data, and the Internet of Things are too strong to overcome. Moreover, because it is a force for good, perhaps a major step along our evolutionary journey, it makes no sense to oppose them. The only reasonable choice is to yield to our digital future and embrace it enthusiastically.

One can understand why this would appeal to Silicon Valley leaders and their gurus. The merger of people and machines, whether it is called the singularity or transhumanism, supports practically everything Big Tech stands for. Make no mistake about it, this is more than a belief system for members of the libertarian tech elite like Elon Musk and Peter Thiel. The new religion of technology, the singularity and transhumanism, has attracted a wider range of congregants, including those who once believed in a more conventional god. Writing in the *Guardian* newspaper, Meghan O'Gieblyn, once firm in her Christian faith, summarizes a decade in the church of transhumanism that followed on her reading of Kurzweil's *The Age of Spiritual Machines*: "But if anything had become clear to me, it was my own desperation, my willingness to spring at this largely speculative ideology that offered a vestige of that first religious promise. I had dis-avowed Christianity, and yet I had spent the past 10 years hopelessly trying to re-create its visions by dreaming about our postbiological future – a modern pantomime of redemp-tion. What else could lie behind this impulse but the ghost of that first hope?"[17]

In at least one other way, the singularity narrative holds considerable importance for understanding the digital world. It reifies technology. For proponents of the myth, technology is a force or a thing that stands opposite to and ultimately controls us. It holds power independent of our capacity to give it form and direction. By diminishing human capabilities and granting independent influence to the Cloud, Big Data, and the Internet of Things, the grand narrative of the singu-larity is, at its core, a sublime justification for accepting what the Next Internet can do for us and pays little attention to the problems they pose or the problems posed by those who see technology differently. These include critics like Raymond Williams, who view technology as a congealed social rela-tionship, or those, like historian David Noble, who define technology as a social construction, if not socially deter-mined. These visions of technology refuse its reification, even as they accept its materiality. Rather than a force opposed to people, they see technology as an instrument of human making, the means by which we create the world and our-selves. Resisting the tendency to technological determinism, this perspective warrants us to use, refuse, and resist technology as we deem best, because we, not technology, and certainly not the collective cloud consciousness, are the only ones capable of doing so.

If the singularity myth tells the story about how we become digital, then the myth of bringing things to life tells the tale of how digital becomes us. In 1973 the General Electric Corporation decided to accept the recommendation of the world-renowned advertising firm BBDO and use the slogan "We bring good things to life" as its primary brand. It worked. In fact it was so successful at shifting the company's image from a purveyor of inexpensive electrical goods to a multinational corporation whose products appealed to the young and the affluent, the saying remained the company brand until 2003. In the mythology of the post-Internet world, "We bring good things to life" may fit better today than ever, but with a change in meaning. GE has become one of the world's leaders in taking things, equipping them with sophisticated sensors, and bringing them, at least in the mythic sense, to life.

COME ALIVE!

For thousands of years, people have told stories about giving life to objects. In the classical myth, Prometheus used clay to fashion humans and gave them the new technology of fire. Mary Shelley's *Frankenstein*, subtitled *The Modern Prometheus* featured the creation of a monster from things found in a lab. These are two of the better known among the many stories featuring the creation of life from ordinary matter. Over the year magicians, conjurers, tricksters, and ordinary people have been portrayed attempting the same feat. All of them mimic the Bible's creation story: "then the Lord God formed a man from the dust of the ground and breathed into his nostrils the breath of life, and the man became a living being." Today, companies and governments invest billions to do what amounts to the same thing. Only, instead of dust, it is the amorphous crystal powder we call silicon. And instead of living, breathing human beings, it is robots that build cars more efficiently than humans can, intelligent systems that drive them more safely than humans can drive them, and drones that kill humans more effectively than humans can kill one other. We give them names like smart car (or smart home, smart city) and weaponized drone. These are the products of the Internet of Things which, when connected to the Cloud and Big Data, perform the ultimate conjurer's trick: they make things come alive. Or as GE would put it: they bring good things to life. It is one of the supreme forms of the sublime.

The promise and the allure of the sublime is that it will lead to transcendence, lifting us out of the banal routine of everyday life. The latter is governed by the babble of words. The former leaves us speechless. Throughout history the sublime has been most often linked to religious exaltation (behold the face of God) and the wonders of the "natural" world, such as towering mountains, majestic canyons and vast oceans. Later, the concept of the natural world was extended to outer space where the Hubble telescope brought visions of a universe spread out over unimaginable distances. Now, in the twentieth-first century, the sublime has become linked to visions of a digitally enabled super intelligence and virtual worlds that open new avenues of transcendence. As with earlier communication technologies, from the telegraph to television, we are in the process of building a mythology around the Internet of Things, infusing it not only with the latest in technology, but also with a narrative vision of the digital sublime.

As the mythology and the magic of creating intelligent things grow, it is useful to remember what happened to the iconic figures that once tried to bring good things to life. For creating life from clay and providing his creation with the gift of fire, Prometheus suffered the wrath of Zeus. The giver of life is chained to a rock and every day, at Zeus's command, an eagle arrives to chew on his liver. The Modern Prometheus did not fare much better as Dr. Frankenstein's creation brought him nothing but pain, heartbreak, and ultimately a terrible death. Most Internet of Things enthusiasts would rather see themselves more like the god of the Christian Bible who used dust to create the human race and, occasional regrets aside, remains faithful to its creation, a sublime manifestation of pure love.

What is arguably the more appropriate mythic analogy to the Internet of Things is the golem, an icon of Jewish folklore. Like the other mythic creatures, golem made the transformation from mud or clay to living being at the hands of religious authorities. But like the Internet of Things, golem are, at best, a mixed blessing. Lacking innate intelligence, they follow instructions by rote and are perfectly obedient. In rare cases they can become uncooperative and, in one instance, this led to a golem's deactivation. When that happened, this particular golem, having grown to enormous size, crushed its creator. The golem appears at first to be far from the story of sublime magic. However, such a conclusion reveals at best an incomplete grasp of what is meant by the sublime. As Edmund Burke, one of the foremost early theorists of the sublime concluded, although beauty invokes pleasure and identification, the sublime is terrifying, awe-inspiring and forces one to grapple with the unknown and the unknowable in nature. The beautiful describes what is pretty and attractive; the sublime summons shock and awe. The sublime arouses not only transcendent bliss beyond speech. It also conjures terror. Such are the golem, prime exemplars of the sublime mixed blessing, representing all those who come alive with uncertain consequences for themselves and their creator. That may be why Karel Capek who coined the term "robot" in his 1921 play R.U.R. or Rossum's Universal Robot is thought to have modeled his creation, arguably the first robot, after the golem. He was equivocal on the point but the plot details are right out of golem mythology.

Today's robotic devices, upgraded with sensors and connected to the global networks of the Internet of Things are also obedient followers of their preset programming to build machines in factories, drive cars autonomously, manage traffic flows, order more milk when we need it, and kill on the orders of someone thousands of miles away. Having driven hands free in a Tesla on an L.A. freeway, I can understand the sublime feeling of watching the car change lanes with no hands on the steering wheel. But sublime excitement can also quickly turn into terror when this modern golem fails to carry out its orders because systems break down or because someone else, the hacker-trickster, for example, steals control. Then cars crash, assembly lines fail, roads fill with anarchy, weaponized drones attack the wrong people, and personal information flows in the wrong direction. The thrill of coming alive turns into damage, destruction, and, sometimes, even death. The golem reminds that the wonder of coming alive can quickly dissolve into the terror of destruction.

Myths featuring the singularity and bringing things to life pervade the culture of the Next Internet. They are a cultural force in the post-Internet world. As such, their compelling tales not only provide a source of meaning and understanding, they also gloss over the significant problems the Next Internet can help create. Chapter five has more to say about these problems.

CHAPTER 5

PROBLEMS

Questioning the ostensibly unquestionable premises
of our way of life is arguably the most urgent of
services we owe our fellow humans and ourselves.
— Zygmunt Baumann

The original Internet was not without problems. But it
benefited from disorganization and decentralization. These
provided room for diversity, including the growth of a public
interest and activist community that was able to make
inroads in support of equality and democracy. Chapter six
addresses their work in the context of considering alternatives
to the Next Internet. Before doing so, it is important to take
up emerging problems. These flow primarily from the singular drive to commercialize, commodify and militarize the digital world. Along with serious environmental, privacy and
labor issues, there is no shortage of significant challenges that
arise from the convergence of the Cloud, Big Data and the
Internet of Things.

COMMERCIALISM AND CONCENTRATION

Hyperbole comes naturally to most discussions about new technology and especially about whatever happens to be the Next New Thing in communication and information technology. Nevertheless it is hard to exaggerate the considerable strength, if not global dominance, of U.S. companies in the digital world. This raises two significant problems. First, the Next Internet is governed almost entirely by commercial principles that define what is good by success in a marketplace dominated by American companies. Second, the power to shape the Next Internet is concentrated among a handful of firms, primarily Apple, Google, Microsoft, Amazon and Facebook.

The dominance of American Next Internet companies makes it very difficult for most nations, with the possible exception of China, to develop independent information systems that can consistently avoid American corporate filters and, particularly, their interest in maximizing profit through commercialism and the commodification of personal identity. China is able to maintain some degree of independence from the American mediasphere only through strong measures of its own that filter out some, but not all American influence. Alternatives to the hegemony of profit and the ability to commodify everything have practically disappeared. The tsunami of deregulation that marked the neo-liberal era swept away state-owned companies and regulatory systems put in place to temper the excesses of the marketplace, such as monopoly and commercialism, and defend the principles of universality and service in the public interest. We are all users, consumers and audiences before we are citizens. The right to communicate has become an opportunity to participate in commercial communication for a price. The real singularity is not the mythic dream of human—machine merger.

It is capitalism whose triumph has meant great success for a handful of companies that have produced remarkable and, some would say, sublime technological innovations. The inventor of the original Internet did not expect it to go this way.

On the occasion of the twenty-eighth anniversary of the Internet, Tim Berners-Lee, now widely considered the Internet's founder, spoke out in disappointment about the state of his invention. Although not as vitriolic, his remarks were reminiscent of those made by Lee de Forest, whose invention of the three-element vacuum tube contributed to his designation (some say self-designation) as the "father of radio." Once optimistic about the public service potential of his creation, de Forest grew deeply frustrated because, in his view, it had succumbed to commercialism. He made his views abundantly clear in an open letter to the 1946 meeting of the National Association of Broadcasters: "What have you done with my child? You have sent him out in the streets in rags of ragtime, tatters of jive and boogie woogie, to collect money from all and sundry for hubba and audio jitterbug. You have made of him a laughing stock to intelligence ... you have cut time into tiny segments called spots (more rightly stains) wherewith the occasional fine program is periodically smeared with impudent insistence to buy and try."[18] De Forest went on to summon high hopes for television and then watch them dashed by commercialism once again.

For Berners-Lee, notwithstanding more reserved language, the problems are similar. For him, an invention that promised greater control over our own data has instead taken away control. Companies provide content in exchange for our personal information, which is packaged and sold to third parties without our knowledge and with terms and conditions that make a mockery of consent. Even our information searches, which once led us, however less conveniently, to a curated reference book or an encyclopedia, now take us to an advertiser-sponsored site run by a private company that processes search results through a commercial filter. Moreover, an invention that offered unprecedented potential to make information accessible to everyone has instead made it easier to spread misinformation. Most people now get their news and information from a handful of social media sites and search engines that choose what to show us based on algorithms developed from the constant harvesting of our personal information. Finally, Berners-Lee argues, an invention that was to advance political participation and democracy has instead made use of political advertising to foster fake news and to keep people from voting. When a political advertising company can customize feeds of real and fake news based on the personal information provided by users, it is much more difficult for voters to develop the knowledge they need to make informed decisions. The potential for manipulation grows at the expense of democracy. These problems are rooted in a system dominated by a handful of platforms that use sophisticated algorithms to manage user behavior. So concerned is Berners-Lee that he established the Web Foundation to address these problems, primarily by expanding public oversight and regulation of the Internet.

Commercialism and commodification are central features, and central problems of the Next Internet. So too is concentration. With monopoly power over key elements of the Next Internet, as well as strengths in all three primary systems, Apple, Google, Microsoft, Amazon and Facebook have reached levels of control that make competition difficult, if not impossible, to achieve. Indeed, their power is so great that they contribute significantly to the growth of inequality. This arises from the ability of monopoly companies to secure returns on their investments well beyond what they would if markets were competitive. These monopoly rents keep profits high and competitors at bay. For example, competitors face major challenges succeeding against Apple's leading position in the hardware and app markets. Similarly, Google dominates search, Microsoft controls the office software market, Amazon has overwhelming influence over Cloud Computing and general retail industries, especially book publishing, and Facebook rules social media. These companies do face competitors, including one another in some markets. However, each has substantial enough holdings in numerous sectors to enable them to use cross-subsidies, predatory pricing, government lobbying and advertising to minimize competitive threats. In effect, having colonized home, work and play, it appears that the only substantial competitive threat they face is sleep, itself made more difficult by the temptation to check the phone when nights turn restless. To have one company dominate at every critical point in the production and distribution of information in the United States and in many parts of the world is a serious problem. To have all five companies poised to control the Next Internet is a fundamental threat to democracy.

The inventor of the Internet is warranted in his worries, but in light of this degree of concentrated corporate power, if anything, he understates the cause for concern. In addition to the problems Berners-Lee correctly raises, these companies have established models for working in the global economy that promote low wages, exploitation and precariousness. The exception is a well-publicized sliver employed in the U.S. offices of the Big Five. But even Google, which business publications regularly recognize as the top company in the United States to work for, is having serious problems at the top, especially for women. In April 2017, the U.S. Department of Labor singled out the firm for "very significant discrimination against women in the most common positions at Google headquarters." This includes wage discrimination. According to the federal agency: "We found systemic compensation disparities against women pretty much across the entire workforce."[19] It appears that one can add exceptional discrimination to the list of exceptional qualities for those employed at Google headquarters. This is hardly a model to strive for in the post-Internet economy but it is sadly characteristic of what has been called the "bro culture" that dominates Silicon Valley.

The U.S. government has done nothing to curtail or regulate the concentration of power at the top of the Next Internet industry. In fact, under the presidencies of Bill Clinton, George W. Bush and Barack Obama, government encouraged and indeed courted Big Tech. For example, it was President Clinton who in 1998 signed into law the Internet Tax Freedom Act, which barred any government, federal, state or local, from imposing Internet-specific taxes. That gave a huge boost to Amazon's monopoly because it enabled the company to eliminate a tax on books that brick and mortar booksellers were required to collect. Partly as a result of what amounts to a government subsidy, most of which went to Amazon, 2300 independent bookstores and the entire Borders chain went out of business between the law's passage and 2015. This tax break also benefited the growth of Apple's iTunes and other online paid music-streaming services as 3100 record stores closed over the same period. Some might suggest that their demise was inevitable but there is no doubt that Clinton's massive tax subsidy, which continued under Bush and Obama, speeded their decline and cemented monopolies for Amazon and Apple. Google, Facebook, Apple and others have also benefited from another huge government tax subsidy permitting them to charge expenses from units in high-tax countries, such as the United States, and to assign income to subsidiaries, some of which engage in no productive activity, based in low-tax countries. This version of corporate welfare, which has thrived in both

Democrat and Republican administrations, is estimated to cost the U.S. treasury $60 billion a year. Nothing in the early period of the Trump Administration gives the impression that this approach will change. If anything, the assault on the few pro-consumer measures the Obama government put in place suggests that the problem will grow worse.

The U.S. government has not always failed to address concentrated corporate power. Throughout its history, but especially beginning with the breakup of John D. Rockefeller's monopoly at Standard Oil, the United States has launched numerous attacks on corporate concentration. Often reluctantly and not always with enthusiasm, the government has led successful antitrust cases against the major television networks, AT&T, Microsoft and other key institutions in the media and information technology industries. There have also been times when the mere threat of antitrust action has led to closer adherence to the law, to greater competition and to the fostering of innovation. But not since 2001, when the Justice Department reached a settlement with Microsoft, has there been a case brought against the Big Five, nor is there evidence that one has been threatened. In spite of their dominance in specific sectors and in the converging systems that make possible the Next Internet, the five leading firms in new media and information technology have not attracted the attention of law-enforcement authorities. No charges of predatory pricing; no charges of restraining trade; no antitrust violations at all. Instead they are able to use their influence over government to shelter revenues in tax havens outside the United States and thereby sharply limit their tax liability. When the dominant tech companies argue that such behavior is entirely legal, they are correct. But the laws they refer to remain in place because of the political and economic power their monopoly profits enable them to wield.

One cannot say precisely why the government has not tried to address the concentration of power in a handful of firms. However, one definite consequence is that U.S. hegemony over the global political economy of the post-Internet world has strengthened. Yet, even those who see this as a net gain, have cause for concern about the political consequences. For example, its monopoly position in social media has enabled Facebook to become the major distributor of journalism in the United States and in much of the rest of the world. Google's control over search and its position as a news aggregator give it similar power. Yet, neither firm employs editors, or reporters or anyone even resembling a journalist. Facebook once did, but scrapped its entire newsroom. The company has actually established a journalism certification program but all it does is teach journalists how to use the social media site effectively. In both Google and Facebook, algorithms based on personal information provide what passes for editing and curation. Rather than pay editors trained in their craft and operating in public, they employ proprietary algorithms deployed to maximize revenue. There is no public participation in their development and no transparency or public accountability for the companies that use them.

The results have been predictable. Facebook has broadcast the live stream of a mentally disabled young man tied up, gagged and attacked with a knife. This was followed by the live stream of two Chicago teenage boys broadcasting their gang-rape of a teenage girl. In March 2017 three even more horrifying videos appeared on Facebook over a 13-minute period. In the first, 37-year-old Steve Stephens announces his intention to murder someone. The second documents him carrying out the deed on a 74-year-old man walking along a street, minding his own business. The final video contains Stephens' confession. Facebook removed the videos after it was notified, but not until many people had watched them. The company gave no indication that these acts would change its policies and practices. Instead, the company's CEO Sheryl Sandberg declared that her company is "not an arbiter of the truth." Appalled, one journalist concluded that "any normal company that had a product capable of producing such toxic outcomes would shut it down and write off the costs." But rather than do that, Facebook continued to boast about its new broadcast service two days after the shooting took place: "Since rolling out Facebook Live, we've seen people and publishers around the world seize the opportunity to share their experiences as they happen, especially during key cultural moments. We've been inspired by the creativity we've seen."[20]

Google is equally emphatic about its reliance on machine learning and artificial intelligence. In the midst of a 2017 crisis arising from the placement of mainstream advertising on hate sites, its chief business officer insisted: "The problem cannot be solved by humans and it shouldn't be solved by humans."[21] The reason is that Google does not want to pay the labor costs that genuine journalism operations have relied on for years. Instead, it hires part time workers through a temp service to make judgements about whether a site was sufficiently bad to warrant no advertising in order to train machine systems and develop algorithms that will replace human assessors in the future. These "ad-raters" disagreed with the company's strategy when they spoke, without Google's authorization, to *Wired* magazine. According to one, "We raters train AI, but we know very well that human eyes – and human brains – need to put some deliberate thought into evaluating content."[22] It is not surprising that workers would complain about training machines to replace them, but their comments were revealing about the rating process itself. In keeping with a company that values low wage labor, Google emphasizes volume of work and speed of completion over accuracy. For example, it routinely asks workers to rate hours-long videos in less than two minutes.

The sad consequences of a focus on maximizing revenue over accuracy are predictable, even for what has been called the gold standard in digital search. If you were to turn to Google in December 2016 and ask "Did the holocaust happen?" the top search result was a site that boasted "The ten reasons why the holocaust didn't happen" provided by the holocaust denier organization Stormfront, which appears to have mastered the not terribly challenging art of gaming the search algorithm. If, at about the same time, you turned to Google again and typed "Are women" into the search box, the first response was to complete the request with the word "evil" and take you to a site that explained how "Every woman has some degree of prostitute in her. Every woman has a little evil in her... Women don't love men, they love what they can do for them. It is within reason to say women feel attraction but they cannot love men."[23] Moreover, those using Google Home, the company's entry in the digital assistant market, would hear a woman's voice repeating the same answer. And since Google controls about 80 percent of desktop search and 96 percent of mobile search, such results would be the ones students, parents and anyone else would likely come across almost everywhere in the world. The presumption of accuracy is seriously misplaced and we have no idea just how badly because there is no independent system of search engine evaluation in place.

Notwithstanding the many imperfections that have marked the history of journalism, for the first time, audiences and readers have no means of knowing how or why news reaches them. Moreover, even though more data is gathered about them than ever before, they have no way of knowing, and therefore no control over, what happens to that information. In addition, they have no way of knowing, and therefore no opportunity to challenge, the ways that news is manipulated for political purposes. Meanwhile the publishers who produce this information are as clueless as their readers and audiences about who they are reaching and how. Armed with their algorithms, social media companies are in control and the public is no longer in any position to judge the credibility of the information Facebook, Google and others propagate.

It should therefore come as no surprise that journalism is in crisis and not just because social media firms have siphoned off the advertising revenue that has traditionally nourished journalism. That Facebook and Google control two-thirds of all digital advertising and over 85 percent of all new digital ads is a serious problem for achieving any semblance of media diversity in a system dependent on advertiser support. Journalism is also in crisis because these companies have been responsible for the massive global proliferation of propaganda, fake news, political manipulation and hateful racist and sexist material that they use to sell advertising. In the absence of meaningful standards, those with power and skill now game the digital news and information system for political gain to an unprecedented degree. Gaming also extends to the sophisticated digital manipulation that goes into creating a favorable news "event." According to the former editor of Canada's major national newspaper, we are on the cusp of Fake News 2.0: "By Canada's next federal election {2019}, a combination of artificial intelligence software and data analytics built on vast consumer surveillance will allow depictions of events and statements to be instantly and automatically tailored, manipulated and manufactured to the predispositions of tiny subsets of the population. Fact or fabrication may be almost impossible to sort out."[24] Aside from the more egregious problems facing journalism, as a result of concentrating power in two companies that have no journalism expertise, there is the challenge of trying to maintain standard day-to-day practices when there is enormous pressure to modify them for a digital world. For example, according to one assessment of the industry, "By offering incentives to news organizations for particular types of content, such as live video, or by dictating publisher activity through design standards, the platforms are explicitly editorial."[25]

These fundamental changes to the news landscape have contributed in no small degree to 2017's major political explosions: Brexit and the election of Donald J. Trump. They have also led to major political protests and calls to do something about the problems facing journalism. Demands for big changes at Facebook and Google have been a major feature of the debate. But given their power, and without the threat of government action, there is little that the two companies feel compelled to do. Meager changes intended to placate critics and polish their image have done almost nothing to diminish propaganda, fake news and political manipulation. Moreover, their insistence on relying on artificial intelligence systems over human editors, primarily because the latter are more expensive, demonstrates a lack of commitment to doing anything substantial. The firm Cambridge Analytica, which advised the Trump campaign on how to work the social media ecosystem, is now a model for political campaigns everywhere. The company boasts that it has combined personality tests with data mined from social media to produce "psychographic profiles" or predictive personality models, for every adult in America. The impact of manipulation is potentially devastating for journalism and for democracy. In the face of this threat to both journalism and democracy, there is no greater evidence of their power than that Facebook and Google continue to do little or nothing and face no significance consequences for their lack of meaningful action. Yes, they have disrupted an industry. But more importantly they have disrupted the democratic process in the United States and in the numerous other nations where they dominate news, information and digital communication.

HEAVY BUGSPLAT AND CYBER WARFARE

Among the many things I have learned from 30 years of research on the military role in the information technology industry, three stand out. First, whenever a new technology, or a new use of an old one, comes along, media tend to focus on civilian applications, and typically benign ones, rather than on how the military may or, more likely, is already using the technology. So when media stories take up drones, it is likely the story will be about whether Amazon will use them for package delivery rather than about how they are already used every day to target insurgents and, all too often, end up killing civilians. Or how America's enemies, including ISIS, made effective use of drones on the battlefield of Raqqa in Syria. Second, when media do take up the militarization of the digital world, they concentrate on how adversaries of the West are using the technology for disruptive and destructive purposes, for example, how China and Russia are hacking Western computers. Rarely do media conclude that it is likely happening both ways, even though the United States has carried out many similar attacks against these nations. Finally, although the U.S. military is the single largest user of computer communication, experts who study media and new communication technology tend to ignore the military in favor of examining social media, sometimes critically but more often the benign, banal and utopian features of new media.

Over the years, a handful of media scholars have paid some attention to the military, including Herbert Schiller, Anthony Oettinger, Dan Schiller, Marcus Breen and Patricia Mazepa, but most, including some of the most critical, pay it little to no regard. As a result many tend to see the digital world as benign. They view disruptions as welcomed innovations and identify digital transgressions only with deviant hackers or with adversaries of the West. But not all disruptions bring progress. Consider this one. A family in Pakistan prepares to celebrate the holy day of Eid, which one member describes as a "magical time filled with joy." To their sudden shock, a U.S. weaponized drone streaks across the blue sky. Eventually, it fires several times sending celebrants to hospital and the family matriarch, 67-year-old Momina Bobi, to her grave. Her son described Momina as the "string that held our family together. Since her death the string has been broken. We feel alone and we feel lost." No terrorist died that day. It was just another case, all too sadly familiar to those who know weaponized drones, of automated warfare gone horribly awry.[26]

It is not known exactly who was targeted and, if it were not for a dissident Congressman who brought what remains of the family to a Washington hearing, the attack would have disappeared from history. Countless other civilian drone strikes in Pakistan, Yemen, Afghanistan, Somalia and elsewhere in what has become a global automated battlefield simply fade into oblivion. In one sense, villagers who came to the family's aid following the attack were fortunate because this was not a "double-tap" strike, one where a drone follows a kill by remaining in the air to target rescuers or returns later to attack the funeral. In fact, repeat drone strikes have become so common that medical aid workers commonly wait hours before providing assistance and people have stopped attending funerals.

It is also not known why the strike took place. What is known is that a global Next Internet system combining electronic surveillance and algorithmic decision-making provided a distant commander, likely an intelligence agency official, with the probability of an efficient kill. If the odds are sufficiently in favor of success, the order goes out to a "pilot" operating from what looks like a trailer half a world away who "flies" the drone and "fires" its lethal weapons. Perhaps it was what the military calls a "signature" strike. That happens when a surveillance system detects the signs of what might be considered hostile activity, such as three men doing jumping jacks, which one State Department official described as the signature of a terrorist camp. Or perhaps it was a group of men loading fertilizer onto a truck, which may be the sign of bomb-making or, just as likely, a group of farmers at work.

Much of this is lost on Westerners beguiled by the latest in "gear" and by talk of smart homes, driverless cars and other wonders of artificial intelligence and the Next Internet. For some, as Chapter 4 documented, it is also the promise of immortality as the Singularity draws near and humans evolve into a machine-enabled super race. For most people, drones are toys or delivery robots, not the instruments of mayhem for thousands of civilians killed or wounded in automated attacks, what the military infamously calls "heavy bugsplat." According to the government's own statistics, President Obama approved 542 strikes killing 3797 people in non-battlefield settings where American forces were not directly engaged, mainly in Pakistan, Yemen and Somalia.

Aside from the importance of understanding the role of weaponized drones in what reputable experts in international law view as possible U.S. government war crimes, drones are among the key instruments in the trend of remote warfare, which involves attacking the enemy without risking one's own troops and material resources. The acceleration of this tendency is extraordinary. Over half of all pilots the Air Force trains operate drones and the share of remotely piloted aircraft in the U.S. fleet rose from 5 percent in 2005 to 31 percent in 2012. Nothing appears to be slowing this growth, not the publicity around civilian casualties, not the high incidence of crashes, nor the mounting evidence of mental health issues among drone pilots whose return home to family after a day of killing precisely-observed and targeted people, including children, is proving difficult to manage. Drones are chosen because they are relatively inexpensive, more agile than piloted aircraft, are effective killers and do not endanger U.S. flying forces. Preparing for a time when even the remote pilot will be eliminated, the military is investing heavily in drones run entirely by AI systems.

Drones are one of the primary instruments for integrating the military into all facets of the Next Internet. There are massive military requirements for the success of this project. While the Air Force has formal control over the U.S. drone fleet, it is the CIA that leads in the key areas of surveillance, intelligence gathering and most importantly, kill decisions. As surveillance and intelligence take a leading role in military decisions, the Agency's role as a top spy is evolving. With each drone strike that its data and decision-making set in deadly motion, the CIA is becoming a major paramilitary organization. This is partly a result of blurring the distinction between analytics and action. Sophisticated algorithms based on Big Data Analytics bridge the two and the CIA tops any branch of the military at this.

To advance the shift from human to data-driven intelligence gathering and algorithmic decision-making, the CIA created the Directorate for Digital Information in 2015, the first new Directorate opened at the Agency since 1963. In order to carry out this new mission, the Agency requires massive data storage and processing capabilities. That is why in 2014 it agreed to pay $600 million to Amazon's cloud computing subsidiary, Amazon Web Services, for remote data storage and processing. The decision thoroughly integrated the Agency into the highest levels of the commercial cloud computing industry and helped catapult Amazon into its leadership. One would think that the tight connection between a world-leading company and the U.S. intelligence establishment would be the subject of critical investigation. It is not.

Moreover, while there has been a bit more public attention on the National Security Agency (NSA), owing primarily to Edward Snowden's revelations about the Agency's indiscriminate surveillance, not much attention has been paid to its role in the development of Cloud Computing, nor to the NSA's intimate ties to the major commercial tech companies. To pursue its mission in Cloud Computing, the NSA has constructed one of the world's largest data center facilities in the mountains of Utah where security is so tight that one of the only clear photographs of the facility was produced by a Greenpeace blimp that flew over to call attention to the secretive surveillance facility. By the NSA's own admission, the Utah facility consumes enough electricity to power 65,000 homes and requires 1.5 million gallons of water for cooling servers every day.

The NSA has cultivated ties to all of the major information technology companies, as Edward Snowden's revelations demonstrated. That many of these ties remain was made clear in October 2016 when we learned that Yahoo followed up a revelation that weak security exposed 500,000 accounts to hackers, by admitting that it also cooperated with the NSA to create software that scanned emails using the company's servers. Strengthening the NSA's hand was the formation in 2009 of the U.S. Cyber Command, which centralized military use of computer communication to attack the digital assets of other nations. A good example of just such an attack was the joint U.S.–Israeli strike on Iran's nuclear research facility using the Stuxnet virus. The attack destroyed centrifuges that it was believed produced enriched uranium for Iran's nuclear weapons program. The modest initial attack intensified in 2010 when, according to U.S, intelligence sources, Israel, dissatisfied with the results, stepped it up in a way that infected computers around the world. These included those of the U.S. Department of Homeland Security, which was never informed about the attack and presumed it was terrorism. Moreover, Iran retaliated with destructive cyber-attacks on oil facilities in Saudi Arabia and on major Western banks. The first battle in the new terrain of cyber warfare was revealing. Iran's nuclear program was delayed, but by only a year. The combined U.S.–Israeli attack also served as a major recruiting tool for Iran's new Cyber Army, which led the retaliatory attacks. Moreover, the U.S. government launched a major cyber-military operation without informing its own leading domestic security agency. Failing to learn from these errors, the U.S. government invested even more authority in the NSA.

The powerful Cyber Command now answers to the NSA head and, while there is a heated debate within the U.S. national security establishment about the wisdom of connecting the two in what are called "dual hat activities," there is little doubt that the intelligence establishment now leads the country's digital military activities. This is a dangerous development for all the reasons that unchecked power always poses major risks. In the absence of an opposing voice, the NSA will continue to develop cyber weapons that have already created unintended consequences. Most prominently, on two occasions in 2017, hackers using software developed by NSA for Stuxnet and other attacks on Iran reconfigured it to unleash major strikes against institutions around the world. Digital assets can find their way to hackers with relative ease, creating havoc for the nations that cyber warfare was intended to protect.

Drones are a key piece in the militarization of the Next Internet. Yet when the U.S. Department of Commerce produced the Obama Administration's official position on the Internet of Things, the only mention of drones was in the context of their advantages for domestic safety: "the potential benefits of a robust IoT environment to improve public safety are well documented across law enforcement, fire services, emergency medical services, and homeland and border security. Wearable sensors, body cameras, drones, and Global Positioning System (GPS) trackers are a few examples of technologies being deployed in the field today. Such devices will increase situational awareness to save lives, improve operational efficiency to lower costs, and enable predictive analytics to identify future public safety situations. Additionally, the proliferation of sensors and predictive analytics used by public safety practitioners will benefit citizens by providing real-time access to better information before disaster strikes, which will help people stay safe in emergencies."[27] The report completely ignores weaponized drones and offers an entirely unwarranted positive vision of the Internet of Things. You would not know it by reading the report, but every technology it describes is shrouded in controversy and none more so than predictive analytics. Big Data makes it tempting to think one can predict criminal tendencies within a community or an individual. However, the confidence it inscribes is not well-placed. Instead, by highlighting the connection between race and crime, predictive analytics has mainly deepened racial tensions in minority communities, promoted racial profiling and damaged individuals whose expected criminal tendencies did not prove accurate.

Alongside the commodification of the Next Internet, we have growing militarization, exemplified in the weaponized drone, the expansion of automated warfare, the deepening power of the intelligence agencies in the new Cyber Command and, significantly, the growing impact of military technology and military approaches on domestic civilian management and control. Whether used for commercial or military purposes, the Cloud, Big Data and the Internet of Things also have significant environmental consequences.

ENVIRONMENTAL IMPACT

Because the digital world is made up of invisible electrons zipping through the air, there is a tendency to view it as immaterial and therefore of little negative consequence for the environment. This is not the case and the sooner the material nature of the Next Internet is recognized, the more likely the environmental problems associated with data centers and Internet of Things devices will be addressed. Next Internet systems require enormous supplies of energy, especially because they are expected to operate nonstop. Backup systems, like diesel generators and lead acid batteries are called on when the primary electricity grid fails or when it is more convenient or cheaper to use backups. These tend to be highly polluting. Moreover, racks of servers, the brains of data centers, can easily overheat. As a result, they have an insatiable need for cooling systems that consume energy and make great demands on water supplies. Finally, there is the problem of e-waste. Whether it is the aging data center, the tens of thousands of servers contained within, or the millions of sensor-equipped "smart" devices, all Next Internet systems eventually break down and give way to new generations of server systems and devices. This seemingly never-ending cycle of deploying the next new thing creates an enormous waste disposal problem, especially for China and the rest of the non-Western world where most e-waste is dumped. Since even e-waste contains valuable metal, including gold, silver, copper, selenium and mercury, it has become a source of income for the desperately poor who scavenge through old servers, computers, hard drives and sensors to find the few valuable bits of gold and other metals that might bring their next meal. However, the hardware that powers the Next Internet also contains highly toxic substances such as lead, mercury, cadmium, tin and bromide dioxins. As a result, poisoning is another major risk facing the poor, their water supply and the land they live on in the post-Internet world. China is not only home to its own Next Internet firms, it also contains the greatest concentration of e-waste in the world. Western tech companies may have a hard time cracking into China's markets, but the waste they produce is a common sight throughout rural China.

Cloud data centers are very material structures and, as they come to fill the world, they produce major environmental policy issues. Proponents of these digital factories argue that data centers can actually advance environmental sustainability by centralizing data storage and processing in large facilities that make much more efficient use of server capacity than do much smaller in-house facilities. The latter have to be plugged in and kept running even when they are not processing data. As a result, server utilization rates run between 10 and 15 percent of capacity. On the other hand the consolidation of IT facilities that the Cloud enables can achieve rates of 80–90 percent, thereby enabling major energy savings especially for small businesses that use their own IT facilities only sporadically. While savings are less substantial for medium and large businesses because their in-house facilities have higher utilization rates (approaching 30–60 percent),

these also carry out their data-processing work more efficiently in the Cloud.

As persuasive as these studies appear, critics note that
most of them are carried out by companies, like General
Electric, that are counting on the Next Internet as a primary
revenue generator for the next several decades. However,
even if we accept that they might arrive with the standard
hyperbole that often accompanies such research, it is not simply a question of challenging self-serving studies. There are
key elements in the environmental impact that are omitted
and two are especially serious. First, these reports do not take
into account the costs of building, maintaining and paying
for the energy use charges on the wired and wireless distribution systems required to connect data centers to users who
will access networks at a considerable distance away from
the places that house and process their data. Cloud data centers may be more efficient than local IT facilities from the
storage and processing perspective, but they are not more
energy efficient at distribution. Consequently, even if companies manage to increase renewable energy sources for cloud
data centers, significant environmental problems will remain.
That is because most access takes place through wireless networks that consume enormous amounts of energy. In fact,
these networks are considerably less efficient at energy consumption than are the data centers that have come in for the
most criticism.

In addition to ignoring distribution costs, reports on
energy savings from the Cloud do not account for the growth
in demand that the Cloud industry needs to keep revenue
flowing. Needing to fill data center capacity, companies, from
Amazon to Rackspace, encourage individuals and organizations to move to the Cloud. While constructing a Cloud data
center is not the same as building a highway, there is a com-
parable process at work. Highways were once considered the

answer to street congestion. Billed as more efficient at handling the growing number of automobiles, they have resulted in the massive expansion in demand for highways because they facilitated development at growing distances from the urban core. Instead of building public transport systems that have proven efficient for the long-term, governments offered incentives to create highway systems that, while providing short-run efficiencies, have turned out to be inefficient on both transport and environmental grounds. Similarly, the unrelenting construction of large cloud data facilities may enhance internal operating efficiencies in the short term, but they will likely expand demand for data services whose storage and processing, while out of the public view, will continue to put pressure on communication networks and on both the built and natural environments. Most reports expect massive expansion in Cloud data center workloads. Some of this growth will result from companies transitioning to the Cloud, as they shrink their in-house facilities. But much of it will also follow from the anticipation of a major spike in data storage, processing and use. According to Cisco, global in-house facilities will expand from 827 exabytes (1 exabyte = 10^{18} bytes) in 2015 to 1.2 zettabytes (1 zettabyte = 10^{21} bytes) in 2020 while cloud centers will grow from the 2015 total of 3.8 zettabytes to 14.1 zettabytes in 2020.

So far, the larger cloud companies have used their economic power and the allure of promised jobs to successfully pressure local governments to provide property tax breaks, cut-rate power deals and relief from environmental regulations. Some firms have responded to opposition from environmental groups, especially Greenpeace, by incorporating solar and other sustainable energy sources into their data center power supplies. Moreover, companies are increasingly trying to locate data centers in cooler climates to limit the use of water to keep servers from overheating. This is understandable because, as Amazon has noted, a data center using 15 megawatts of power needs up to 360,000 gallons of water every day for cooling. Facebook learned this lesson early on when its first data center was almost ruined because its servers overheated. As a result, businesses are understandably very mindful of the need to keep their servers running whatever the environmental cost.

They are also mindful of the constant pressure to keep their servers on at all times. Outages, even if only for short periods of time, make the kind of news that companies like Amazon and Facebook do not like to see reported. As a result, they are not reluctant to take extraordinary measures, including the use of heavily polluting and even carcinogenic power sources, if it means keeping users on their sites. Current efforts by Cloud companies are piecemeal at best. Some, like Apple are taking solid steps. Others, Amazon, for example, are not. As data requirements grow, systematic regulation is required, including a broad review of discount power deals, the use of massively polluting backup systems, and the diversion of water resources to cool servers.

Notwithstanding any steps forward in the use of sustainable energy sources for the operation of data centers, a major source of power consumption in the Next Internet comes from operating the sensors embedded in the billions of Internet of Things connected devices and from the communication systems that link people and things through cellular and other wireless networks. A world of ubiquitous, always-on connected devices, is enough to make fossil fuel executives gleeful with anticipation, especially the lobbying arm of the coal industry which views the Next Internet as an opportunity to build on what a study for the U.S. National Academy of Sciences calls "the renaissance of coal."[28] According to a report sponsored by the coal industry, "The inherent nature of the mobile Internet, a key feature of the emergent Cloud architecture, requires far more energy than do wired networks.... . Trends now promise faster, not slower, growth in ICT energy use."[29] When the environmental impacts of Next Internet systems are considered alongside their massive stimulation of consumption, the implications for climate change are staggering to contemplate.

Nevertheless, like the Cloud, the Internet of Things has been hailed for its potential to curtail emissions by making economic processes more energy efficient. A 2013 report produced by a private think tank claimed that if the technology rolled out as anticipated, the gains would be more than large enough for society to meet the goal of stabilizing world climate. Specifically, in the energy sector, the application of Internet of Things technologies to build a "smart grid" could save more than 2 billion metric tons of CO_2e (carbon dioxide equivalent) and facilitate the transition to renewable energy sources. In transportation, Internet of Things devices could save another 1.9 billion metric tons of CO_2e by making ship, truck, air and rail transport more efficient. In the built environment, savings of 1.6 billion metric tons of CO_2e could be achieved by increasing the energy efficiency of cooling, heating, lighting, appliances and security systems. Finally, the same saving could be achieved in agriculture by increasing efficiency in seeding, harvesting, water and fertilizer use, as well as through reductions in deforestation.[30] This and other reports like it demonstrate the potential for major energy savings. However, as with similar reports about the Cloud, they do not take into account the costs of constant communication among devices as well as between them and Cloud data centers. These might be diminished if, as some expect, intelligence devolves from the Cloud to decentralized and distributed Edge computing systems. In effect, these would diminish the distance communication requirements of device to Cloud communication and may actually prove to be essential to achieve efficient response times. But whether Cloud or Edge computing is deployed, the sheer number of active Internet of Things devices guarantees that the already serious issue of e-waste will multiply many times over.

There is no certainty that the forecast growth in Table 1, which estimates that the 20-some billion devices in operation today will grow to over 75 billion by 2025, will prove accurate. Security, compatibility and a host of other issues may derail the expected tripling. Or, it may be the case that advances in artificial intelligence, machine learning and robotics will exceed expectations and Table 1 may underestimate growth. Whatever the outcome, there is little doubt that the demand for power will grow substantially and, along with it, the amount of e-waste. To get some perspective on the expansion of e-waste, we need to start from the recognition that the Next Internet era has just begun to penetrate the most prosperous nations and is making inroads in others, like China. It is hardly a feature of life throughout most of India, despite the country's strong tech sector. In 2016 less than a third of India's 1.3 billion people used the Internet. What if the current push to add another 500 million Internet users to the global grid succeeds to the point where just two-thirds of the population were equipped with mobile devices and began to work alongside robots, navigate smart cities and use Internet-enabled devices in their homes? What if similar campaigns to extend the Next Internet to Africa, Latin America and the rest of Asia were also successful? Some would likely hail this as a major step forward in the expansion of a global information society. But, barring revolutionary developments in energy production, which remain elusive, the spike in energy demand will likely exceed any anticipated savings and will produce many more mountains of e-waste.

Most people in the developed West have very little awareness of the e-waste issue because companies have managed to ship most of it to the developing world, often illicitly. According to a report by the UN Environment Programme, close to 90 percent of the world's e-waste worth about $20 billion is shipped outside the law. Electronic devices like phones, computers, tablets, televisions and accessories that shippers label "used" or "second-hand" turn out, upon inspection, to be non-functioning e-waste.

By 2017, the total annual production of e-waste worldwide reached 50 million metric tons with most of it ending up in Asia and Africa, where much of this is hand recycled by individuals who are directly subjected to the health hazards associated with the toxic metals and chemicals these devices contain. At one facility in Guiyu, China, known as the world's e-waste capital, a so-called informal recycling center had women melting circuit boards over coal fires, subjecting themselves to toxic fumes. Studies have demonstrated that 80 percent of Guiyu's children have more respiratory sickness, higher levels of lead and cadmium toxicity and poorer cognitive performance than children in the surrounding areas. After the UN and international media reported on this, the "informal" system was centralized in an industrial park where conditions improved. Nevertheless, the mountains of waste continue to grow and there is no expectation that they will be reduced anytime soon. According to the leader of one NGO that focuses on the issue, "We'll worry about the massive quantities later, we've got to stop poisoning people."[31]

Some companies have made formal commitments to end e-waste shipments of their products to Asia and Africa. But many of these end up dumped there anyway. One way we know this is because the Basel Action Network and MIT's Senseable City Lab teamed up to embed trackers in devices that one of these companies, Dell, shipped to Goodwill Industries locations in the United States for sale as used devices. Eventually, some of these products ended up in waste facilities located in Hong Kong, mainland China and Thailand. Dell has one of the toughest audit programs in the industry and yet its products continue to fill dangerous mountains of waste overseas. That is because its firm commitment is not backed by the audits of every shipment that would be required to police the process. Shippers can make more money by illegally sending e-waste to Asia and Africa than they can from Dell or any of the other companies who claim that their recycling programs will keep devices from poisoning people in the developing world. In the absence of commitments from all manufacturers to a global system of e-waste monitoring, the problem will become exponentially worse with the arrival of the billions of Internet of Things devices that are powering the Next Internet. Moreover, the expansion of broadband connectivity throughout the world using small earth-orbiting satellites will extend the proliferation of space junk into space. Google, SpaceX, Boeing and Samsung are planning to deploy thousands of devices, what are called satellite constellations, over the next several years in order to operate low-cost broadband networks on earth, and, undoubtedly, will produce additions to the growing mountains of e-waste.

PRIVACY, SURVEILLANCE AND THE INTERNET OF HACKABLE THINGS

From analog through to digital, privacy has been an issue throughout the history of electronic communication. Theft of private telegraph messages was a major worry in the heyday of what has been called the Victorian Internet. Nosey neighbors listening in on the party lines that dominated the early decades of the telephone was a constant privacy issue. Even though broadcasting was intended to reach a mass of people,

privacy remained a concern. Radio was used to send messages to areas with no or limited wired telephony and to span
oceans before submarine cables and later satellites took over
the job of international communication. Moreover, radio and
television brought a vast expansion in commercialism and
state propaganda that many felt left precious little room for
private life. A surge in privacy issues greeted precursors to
the Internet in the 1960s and 1970s. Early cable television
services experimented with "interactive" video that enabled
viewers to choose programs. When an Ohio service was
found to keep a record of viewer selections, including the
choice to view Adult content, an uproar ensued over what
this might do to reputations and careers.

With the arrival of the Internet, privacy became a source
of great concern and that is only likely to deepen with the
expanded connectivity of the Next Internet. These concerns
are understandable but they tend to lack coherence and
breadth. Specifically, the privacy problem tends to be defined
in the negative, as the loss of something that is not easily
defined. Moreover, the problem is almost always viewed in
individual terms, as something specific people lose or gain. It
is taken to be a social problem only to the extent that many
or few individuals retain or lose their privacy. Finally, privacy
debates often center on what to do about the theft of private
data and communication resulting from hacking and other
forms of criminal activity. The focus is on crimes like identity
theft that compromises personal privacy rather than on privacy violations that are the planned consequences of everyday business practices and government surveillance. In order
to best comprehend the seriousness of the privacy issue for
the Next Internet, it is essential that we shift how privacy is
conceptualized and understood.

There is a tendency to treat privacy as the right to be left
alone or as a tradable commodity, something we give up,

such as information about ourselves, to receive something we want, such as access to a social media platform or to email. These are serviceable but also narrow, weak, and tell us little about why privacy is important. They are also almost entirely focused on the individual as the repository of privacy. To deepen understanding of this issue, it is essential to change how we think about privacy. Specifically, we need to see privacy in spatial terms. It is the psychological space that individuals need for self-development and the space that social groups require to form a community. Developing a unique self requires the personal space to experiment, perform different roles, take risks, try out new values, get to know ourselves and ultimately form a coherent personality that, while constantly evolving, contains a core identity. Protecting individual privacy means preserving personal control over this vital space against forces that make the formation of a self-directed personality or integral character more difficult, if not impossible. This is why psychologists increasingly recommend creating a technology-free space. According to one, each of us needs to create "a screen-free space" in their homes by locking "phones and other screens in a drawer in a room far away from where they are for a few hours a day. It's very hard to develop an addiction to something you can't see or reach, so the best thing you can do is spend time away from tech – and spend time in a room that is as near to screen- and tech-free as possible."[32] Social groups need self-governing space as well to develop a coherent and cohesive group identity. One can also lose a collective identity, of a family, a group of friends, or a neighborhood when the sense of community is taken or traded away. Privacy is both spatial as well as social.

Privacy and associated security concerns rise exponentially with the Next Internet because the growth in digital connectivity increases opportunities for both technical breakdowns and criminal hacking. Indeed one tech journalist referred to the Internet of Things as "the greatest mass surveillance infrastructure ever."[33] Yet, we are only in the earliest days of the Next Internet. By the standards anticipated in a digital world where the Internet of Things is fully developed, today's Internet is far from a fully connected world. Only 40 percent of the world's population now uses the Internet at least once a year, and, as one might expect, access is concentrated in the developed world and in urban centers. With only 1 percent connectivity among objects, we are very far from the vision of ubiquitous computing. But even at this relatively low level, technical problems and criminal hacking plague the system. On one chaotic day in 2015, the entire U.S. fleet of United Airlines planes was grounded, the New York Stock Exchange shut down for several hours and the Wall Street Journal's computers simply stopped operating. All of these were explained as the result of technical "glitches." Just as this calamity hit the news stream, the U.S. government reported that hackers had stolen the personnel records of 22.1 million federal employees, contractors and their families and friends who provided information for background checks. The haul also included over one million sets of fingerprints. The British Chamber of Commerce reported that criminal hackers attacked fully one in five of its businesses in 2016 in part because most companies lack even the most basic security protections. Interestingly, it appears that larger companies were more likely than small businesses to experience attacks. With well over a billion of its accounts breached, no attack surpasses those at Yahoo. As of March 2017, in spite of several arrests of Yahoo hackers, one billion of the hacked accounts were still for sale on the open market.

The attack on Yahoo was significant but overshadowed by a ransomware hack in May 2017 that captured data on over 200,000 users in 150 countries. The hackers would not return the data until the victims paid a ransom in bitcoin, the digital currency that is difficult to trace. It was the largest ransomware attack in history and was especially worrisome because it hit very sensitive sites such as the computers that house the personal data of those using the National Health Service of Great Britain. What makes the case even more interesting is that the NSA was responsible for producing the hacking software that led to the attack. NSA used it in the Agency's own cyberwarfare activities, including Stuxnet, and those who carried out the attack repurposed the software. The connection between hackers and intelligence agencies is not unusual. Rather it simply demonstrates that there is a fine line between criminal hacking and what is considered legitimate state activity. Just a month later, the world learned that this was not an isolated incident when hackers struck again shutting down corporate and government systems around the world.

One response to these stories is to single them out as security outliers. Yahoo was just careless with user data; other companies are not. This is wrong. Consider Amazon, the beating heart of retail. Increasingly, hacker criminals posing as third-party sellers are using stolen credentials to post phony deals on the Amazon site and then pocket the cash. Cyber-criminals have been known to hack into the Amazon accounts of sellers who have not used them for a while to post deep discounts on nonexistent merchandise. Third-party sellers now make up over half of Amazon's sales and the company's failure to provide a secure space for deals threatens its position as a market maker. It is also the case that few public cloud computing systems have sufficient security to protect user data. One study reported that 82 percent of all databases stored in the Cloud lacked encryption protection and Amazon Web Services is a major culprit.

It is understandable that such breaches in personal and collective privacy would attract widespread attention. But this is also unfortunate because the amount of coverage tends to obscure the constant daily assaults on privacy that take place well within the law by major businesses, embodying a system best called *surveillance capitalism*, and by government, which is increasingly acting like a *surveillance state*. Indeed, the most significant threats arise from the activities of data-hungry businesses and governments. The greatest attraction of the Next Internet's promise of ubiquitous computing is the valuable data on the behavior of people and the performance of objects. These offer opportunities as businesses refine targeted advertising and product development well beyond the crude systems that today's Internet makes possible and they also provide opportunities for governments to deepen tracking and control of citizen behavior and attitudes. Moreover, they provide employers with new tools to carry out an old process: controlling their employees.

Consider the commercial benefits to insurance companies that will be able to continuously monitor the health of customers, their driving habits and the state of their homes; to credit bureaus that set the data point that determines the ability to borrow the money for a home or car purchase; to governments that can adjust benefits and other services based on citizen behavior registered in their actions, as well as their interactions with one another, and with the things that fill their lives or to employers that, as chapter four reported, are even now requiring office workers to wear sensor devices on and under the skin for ubiquitous performance monitoring. Moreover, occupations as prosaic as trucking now feature dashboard cameras to monitor and capture the labor of drivers.

As earlier chapters have documented, the Big Five tech companies have blazed the trail for surveillance capitalism in the Next Internet. The trio of digital assistants, including Amazon's Alexa, Apple's Siri and Google's Home, has provided unprecedented access to our private lives. With the capacity to send voice commands to the Cloud, these companies do not just help you purchase a book, play a song, or answer a search request. They deliver expressions of our wants and needs, as well as those of partners, children and whoever else happens to be within the reach of these always-on devices to whoever is willing to buy the information. Amazon's product developers receive raw transcripts of Alexa "conversations" to better enable the online giant to produce products tailored to specific markets and specific users. Similarly, Microsoft's Cloud-based suite of Office software captures and markets information on users for its own use and for interested third parties. Rounding out the picture, as Table 3 documents, Facebook provides a seemingly endless stream of data to a global market eager to make profitable use of the bits and pieces of the personal identities and the manifold networks to which users are connected.

Fresh sources of such data gathering are appearing all the time as old technologies like the automobile and the kitchen stove are made "smart," that is, capable of delivering a steady flow of details about our lives. Consider the humble television, which, in the age of computers, tablets and do-everything phones, appeared headed for legacy status, if not the dustbin of history. But it too has been revived and made smart. In this case, smart means capable of responding to voice commands. Whether you buy from Samsung, Sony or LG, for the convenience of enabling a buyer's television to response to vocal demands, the buyer agrees to have those commands uploaded, turned into text and delivered to a third-party company. Legal experts have noted that distinguishing between commands directed at the television and general household conversation can be difficult. Some of

Table 3. A Partial List of Data Facebook and Its Advertisers Gather about Users.

1. Location

2. Age

3. Gender

4. Language

5. Level of education

6. School

7. Ethnicity

8. Income and wealth

9. Home ownership

10. Home value

11. Age of home

12. Size of both home and property

13. Household composition

14. Users with an anniversary within 30 days

15. Friends with someone with an upcoming anniversary, who are newly engaged, married, recently moved, or with an upcoming birthday

16. Users in long-distance relationships

17. Users in new relationships

18. Users with new jobs

19. Users who are newly engaged or recently married

20. Users who have recently moved

21. Users with upcoming birthdays

22. Users' parents

23. Parent types (soccer, trendy, etc.)

24. Users likely political involvement

25. Political ideology (liberal, conservative, socialist, alt-right)

26. Relationship status

Table 3. (*Continued*)

27. Employer

28. Occupation

29. Interests

30. Transportation preference: car, motorcycle, bicycle

31. Users shopping for a car: including make and model

32. Users who bought or are likely to need auto parts or accessories

33. Make, model and age of car owned or leased

34. Year car was bought or leased

35. Users who own small businesses

36. Users who donate, divided by type of donation and by charity

37. Preferred operating system: Mac, Windows, Linux

38. Users who own a game console/play video games

39. Users who create Facebook events

40. Users who manage a Facebook page other than a personal one

41. Users who upload photos to Facebook

42. Preferred Internet browser

43. Preferred email service

44. Views on technology: Early/late adopter

45. Users who are expatriates by country of origin

46. Type of bank used

47. Users who invest by type of investment

48. Credit history

49. Credit card preference

50. Users who carry a balance on their credit card

51. Debit card preference and usage

52. Radio/television usage

53. Favorite television shows

54. Smart phone brand/usage

55. Internet service provider

Table 3. (*Continued*)

56. Coupon users

57. Household occupants clothing preferences

58. Shopping patterns over the year

59. Grocery preferences

60. Users who buy beauty products

61. Users who buy medications, including over-the-counter pharmaceuticals

62. Household product purchases

63. Pet preferences

64. Purchases for pets

65. Extent of online shopping

66. Restaurant preferences

67. Store preferences: small/medium/Big Box

68. Users receptive to online auto insurance, higher education or mortgages

69. Users anticipating a household move

70. Professional sports preferences

71. Users travel preferences

72. Commuting patters

73. Vacation preferences

74. Travel app

75. Users who frequent online vacation sites

Source: Washington Post, August 16, 2016, http://wapo.st/2plxYQG.

what a user says around the home will inevitably be recorded, transcribed and stored in the Cloud. In addition, companies reserve the right to collect information on program choices, the length of time the set is on, and since this is a "smart" device, detailed health information when the buyer uses the set in connection with a fitness program. In addition to sharing information with technical and marketing partners, set manufacturers also retain the right to share data with others who provide users with information on products and services. Although not spelled out in privacy agreements, these often include data brokers, insurance companies and credit bureaus. No major provider of smart televisions provides a limit on the length of time they will retain data. What the agreements are clear about, however, is that nothing in them applies to third-party apps (such as from Netflix) that the user chooses to download.

Alongside surveillance capitalism there is the surveillance state, a term that refers to the processes that governments use to monitor people, including their own citizens, and to insure control over their behavior. The Next Internet enormously expands the surveillance state. Cloud Computing vastly enlarges the capacity to store data whether through a government's own facilities, as is the case with the NSA's massive data center complex in Utah, or through commercial facilities, as the CIA has demonstrated with its use of Amazon's Cloud. As the revelations of former NSA consultant Edward Snowden and others have demonstrated, these agencies are not averse to exceeding legal constraints including those limiting their authority to spy on and build detailed profiles on American citizens. They have indiscriminately captured data on foreign leaders, including allies, and built profiles on foreign citizens, most of whom have no reason to be monitored. These agencies have also not been shy about denying their involvement in these activities, in spite of incontrovertible evidence. They now have near unlimited capacity to store, process and access information on citizens everywhere.

Their work and that of agencies like the Federal Bureau of Investigation as well as local law enforcement are greatly assisted by the growth of Big Data Analytics. In addition to aiding legitimate law enforcement, Big Data enables a disturbing trend in the development and application of algorithms that expand the temptation to let the data "speak for themselves" by making predictions based on information about types of crime, who commits them and where these are committed. What is called "predictive analytics" often reinforces racist and other discriminatory practices that promote mass incarceration of African Americans and other minorities, now with the blessing of data science. Commenting on the development of algorithms using social data, a senior researcher for Microsoft Research New York City concluded, "as long as they are trained using data from society and as long as society exhibits biases, these methods will likely reproduce these biases."[34]

Finally the Internet of Things expands the reach of the surveillance state through weaponized drones and other forms of robotic warfare. Even a sensor-equipped television can serve as a surveillance device. Edward Snowden has described just how the CIA might compromise a smart TV ordered from Amazon before it arrives at the buyer's home: "People say, the CIA's not going to be breaking into my house. That's true − but they don't go into your house. They wait for when these devices are being shipped to you, when you order them on Amazon or whatever. They go to them at the airports, they get the box, they use a little hairdryer to soften the adhesive, they open the box, then they put the USB stick in. They seal the box back up all nice and perfect, and then they ship it on to you. And now your router, your computer, your TV is hacked. This is a very routine thing that happens."[35] With the NSA at the helm of the U.S. Cyber Command and without organized resistance, it is likely that these and other surveillance state practices will greatly expand in the coming years.

AUTOMATION AND JOBS

Between October of 2016 and April of 2017, 89,000 jobs in the U.S. merchandise industry disappeared, equivalent to the size of the entire U.S. coal industry, the example President Trump often cited of an industry left behind by the economic recovery that needed rejuvenation to Make America Great Again. Led by Amazon, e-commerce has expanded rapidly since 2014, leading experts to conclude that in-store shopping has reached a tipping point and is headed for a sharp decline. In the first three months of 2017 nine retail chains in the United States declared bankruptcy and thousands of shops have been shuttered. Visits to shopping malls are down by half and investors have pretty well given up the ghost. Restaurants and entertainment venues once picked up the slack, but observers do not expect this to continue. As a result, the retail collapse has surpassed even the Great Recession of 2008.

Hollowing out large malls and small shopping centers, this transformation is having a profound impact on a society where one in every ten workers is employed in retail. It is becoming increasingly clear that one consequence of the Next Internet and its support for online shopping is an upheaval in one of the major providers of full-time work, especially for women. For them, it is a cruel irony that Amazon, which is one of the primary causes of retail's demise, is building a handful of brick and mortar shops, as if to mock a bygone era, museums to a past that will not likely be recovered. But, some experts argue, it is more complicated. Some of these jobs will be replaced by warehouse work needed to serve the growing hordes of online shoppers. Skeptics about job loss maintain automation is all part of the natural process of creative destruction that, since the time economist Joseph Schumpeter described the concept, has led to the recognition that this is simply part of a healthy economic system. Nevertheless, such assessments provide cold comfort to those who are actually losing their jobs, including many warehouse and retail workers whose jobs have gone to robots. Consider that Walmart is replacing $13 an hour back office cash counting jobs with robots that can count eight bills a second and 3000 coins a minute.

The impact of the Next Internet on jobs and the labor process is an important policy issue. At first glance, it is tempting to think "here we go again" because the impact of technology on jobs has been discussed for many years but especially since the end of World War II when the computer scientist Norbert Wiener generated considerable public debate by raising the specter of massive job loss due to automation. Moreover, the Next Internet is creating, and will likely continue to create, employment, including traditional construction jobs in the build out of global networks of cloud data centers, in the new profession of data science, and in the control, maintenance and monitoring of networked things, including robots. There is another reason why it is important to approach the impact of computer technology on jobs and the economy with caution. As research documents, overall employment has been much more closely tied to a nation's GDP than to computerization and, except for the late 1990s when there was massive investment in hardware, the long-promised productivity gains from IT have failed to materialize.

However, today there are far more opportunities for the new technology to eliminate human labor, including professional knowledge work. In fact, one expert consultant prefers to define Cloud Computing as "nothing more than the next step in outsourcing your IT operations."[36] This is in keeping with a general tendency which one researcher for the private think tank Gartner Associates summarizes succinctly: "The long run value proposition of IT is not to support the human workforce — it is to replace it."[37] The Next Internet creates immediate opportunities for companies to rationalize their information technology operations. Again, from Gartner, "CIOs believe that their data centers, servers, desktop and business applications are grossly inefficient and must be rationalized over the next ten years. We believe that the people associated with these inefficient assets will also be rationalized in significant numbers along the way."[38]

Next Internet companies maintain that their systems can break a pattern in business organizations that began when the first mainframe computers entered the workplace. Back then all business and government agencies insisted that it was essential to operate their own information technology departments and, especially for larger organizations, their own data centers. Next Internet supporters insist that it is no longer essential to build and run thousands of organization-specific facilities when a few large data centers can meet the demand at lower cost with far fewer professional personnel. The savings in labor costs, they maintain, pay for the transition. This process has already begun and early studies demonstrate that, even with limited downsizing of IT departments, companies are saving between 15 and 20 percent of their IT budgets.

The Next Internet also makes possible the widespread rationalization of most creative and information-based labor because the work of these occupations increasingly involves the production, processing and distribution of data. According to one observer, "In the next 40 years analytics systems will replace much of what the knowledge worker does today."[39] A 2013 report concluded that almost half the current U.S. workforce is directly threatened and in the high-risk category for job loss. Whatever the precise share, there is no doubt that the current trend is to use software to shift knowledge worker labor over to machine systems. We are now beginning to see the impacts on education, health care, the law, accounting, finance, sales and the media. Private and public sector organizations are encouraged to outsource all but their core business processes to companies like Salesforce. com which specializes in managing vast databases of customer information, a job that marketing and client service departments contained inside companies once typically performed. We are also seeing this take place at the pinnacle of financial services where the world's largest investment fund company BlackRock began restructuring and eliminating the jobs of some of its top traders in 2017 because many investment decisions are now being made by algorithms. Capital firms like BlackRock are expected to increase their 2017 spending on artificial intelligence systems from $1.5 billion to $2.8 billion in 2021, an investment that will pay off, according to one report, in the loss of 230,000 jobs in capital markets by 2025. At the other end of the Next Internet occupational structure, driverless trucks are expected to decimate what was once a staple of good, full-time, unionized jobs. A 2017 meeting of AI experts forecast that half of all trucks will be driverless within the next 15 years throwing 1.75 million truckers out of work. In addition, they forecast that half the people who now analyze medical records will have been replaced by AI within nine years. Within ten years, 95 percent of air traffic control jobs will be done robotically. In less than 25 years, robots will perform more than half of all surgeries and complete most management tasks at the majority of big companies. Even leaving room for the hyperbole that enthusiastic artificial intelligence experts often bring to their predictions, it is reasonable to conclude that we are in the midst of a massive transformation in labor.

The expansion of outsourcing to computers raises serious questions for the entire global system of flexible production. According to Gartner, "That outcome will hit all economies — especially emerging ones like India that now dominate technology outsourcing."[40] The Next Internet also expands the range of potential outsourcing practices. It may be an overstatement to declare, as did *Forbes* magazine, "We are all outsourcers now," but it certainly makes feasible more kinds: "Outsourcing is no longer simply defined by multi-million-dollar mega-deals in which IT department operations are turned over to a third party. Rather, bits and pieces of a lot of smaller things are gradually being turned over to outside entities."[41] Amazon is a major force in this process with its Mechanical Turk business that charges individuals and organizations to outsource micro-tasks to a worldwide reserve army of online piece workers. Combined with the promise of product warehouses full of robots to locate, pack, and ship goods, and drones to deliver them, Amazon is the leading edge of the Next Internet's push to expand labor intensification throughout the world. It has become a model for companies across many different industries. For example, in 2017, the shoe manufacturer Adidas decided to break with the standard supply chain model in the industry by moving production from Asia to Germany. The reason? Asia is no longer the low-wage, submissive paradise for Western companies. Moreover, Germany has made enormous strides in robotics and Adidas plans to shift from a human to a robot workforce. It is expected that the entire apparel industry, with its army of sewing robots, will follow and lead a major supply chain restructuring that will re-source production without increasing human employment. Given accelerating demand, it is estimated that the world will go from taking 50 years for the first million robots to come into use to eight years for the next million.

It is far from certain what the precise impact of the Next Internet will be for jobs and the quality of work. Mass unemployment is one possibility. So too is a world where those with jobs will have to learn how to work with robots and other forms of intelligent machines. Living labor, as Marx called it, is rapidly being overtaken by the dead labor of machines. As a result, governments, which will pay the price for negative outcomes, are trying to find solutions to what most agree will be one crisis or another that is soon to hit workers throughout the world.

CHAPTER 6

CITIZENSHIP IN A
POST-INTERNET WORLD

The Web as I envisaged it, we have not seen it yet.
The future is still so much bigger than the past.
— Tim Berners-Lee

DESPAIR AND DISRUPTION

Reflecting on the problems emerging in the early days of the Next Internet, one might be forgiven for despairing about the prospects for finding solutions. After all, the Next Internet is thoroughly commercial and led by five companies that exercise unprecedented power throughout the world. One consequence is the growing commodification of our institutions, our bodies and our consciousness. As a result, it is difficult to address the massive environmental problems that the Next Internet is creating. Notwithstanding well-publicized gestures, Big Tech puts serious pressure on the built environment, leaving the world with mountains of toxic e-waste, draws down energy supplies needed to fuel 24/7 connectivity and puts significant stress on water resources essential to keep systems functioning. Governments are doing precious little to address either the power of Silicon Valley or the environmental damage they are creating. That is partly because they are deeply complicit in the ceaseless expansion of the Next Internet. The U.S. and other governments benefit from the construction of a military-information complex with robots and drones serving as profitable killing machines. Moreover, as the prying eyes of surveillance capitalism and the surveillance state penetrate all facets of individual and social life, it is hard to imagine regaining the space that people so desperately need to form an independent identity sufficient to act as autonomous individuals. Finally, never in the history of communication technology has a greater threat been posed to the existence of jobs and the quality of work by the dead labor of robots and artificial intelligence.

As terrifying as this future appears for the vast majority of people, it is also highly unstable because it comes with deepening levels of inequality, environmental devastation and the onset of climate change, militarism, mass surveillance and joblessness. The combination of these and other problems will make it very difficult to maintain the status quo for more than a few years. This is especially the case because the massive concentration of corporate power has already given rise to political parties and leaders whose actions are deepening each of these instabilities. Led by President Trump and the U.S. Republican Party, most constraints on corporate concentration are being removed, including the Net Neutrality regulations that provided some relief from the ability of Big Tech to deepen its hold on the digital world. Climate change deniers are taking charge of environmental policy, including dismantling the Environmental Protection Agency, which, since it was established in the Nixon Administration, has managed to strengthen environmental standards and has helped educate two generations of Americans on the essential need to fight climate change. Massive shifts in government spending directed towards the military mean that mass surveillance and autonomous weaponry have the green light to accelerate their development. Finally, there are few signs that any government is prepared to address the massive job loss that artificial intelligence and robotics are already bringing about. Their only strategy, such as it is, involves using social media and other tools that the Next Internet provides to stir the pot of nationalism, promote anti-immigrant hysteria and publicize a few gestures to return to an industrial past that is long gone.

Nevertheless, it is reasonable to conclude that growing instability will not, in itself, lead to progress in solving seemingly intractable problems. Tech-induced instability is more likely to create massive disruptions, strains and tensions throughout the world. This is especially likely because digital systems are extremely vulnerable to attacks from hackers working alone or aligned with governments and to breakdowns originating in system outages and software engineering errors. Authoritarianism and anarchy are easier to imagine than is democratic social change.

REVENGE OF ANALOG?

One can certainly understand the growing tendency to find solutions to the troubling problems of the digital world in a return to analog forms of communication and culture. Analog is shorthand for the offline world of material objects that operate through direct human contact and not through the mediation of binary code. It is the human hand gripping a pencil and writing on paper or the material grooves in a vinyl record produced to mimic the sounds of music. It is face-to-face human communication. There are numerous books on the subject but David Sax's bluntly titled *The Revenge of Analog* has received the widest attention including a very favorable review by the *New York Times*' top reviewer Michiko Kakutani. Sax finds analog's revenge is the return to popularity of traditional media, including vinyl records, paper journals and notebooks, especially the hipster favorite Moleskine, board games, traditional film and print newspapers and magazines. He also chronicles the rebirth of small retail shops and people-centered workplaces, unstructured play and schools that ban digital devices. No enemy of digital, Sax celebrates digital technologies that make an analog life easier and perhaps even richer. The popular note-taking software company Evernote has, for example, opened its own analog business featuring an Evernote branded Moleskine, Post-it products and other material goods. Amazon is opening retail book outlets, grocery stores and its revival of the *Washington Post* is widely considered a major success. The company's 2017 purchase of the Whole Foods upscale grocery chain is a major step in Amazon's analog strategy. There is some evidence that the turn to analog, while not necessarily a massive upheaval, is genuine. 2016 data from Great Britain indicate that e-book sales dropped by three percent in 2016 with consumer e-book sales plummeting even further, by 17 percent. Meanwhile print books are up by eight percent. Music stores continue to sell more and more vinyl from the growing number of pressing plants. Streaming audio dominates sales but vinyl has undeniably made a comeback. Yet, it is not hard to conclude that analog's revenge, at least as Sax describes it, is limited to demonstrating that there is dissatisfaction with digital. Only the most optimistic of analog enthusiasts believe that vinyl will make a major dent in digital streaming and that board games will challenge the leading video game companies.

Discussions of the analog alternative tend to focus on a handful of fashionable items that vintage enthusiasts covet. One of the exceptions is Sherry Turkle's research that resulted in the book *Reclaiming Conversation*, an investigation of what is arguably the most analog of communication media, face-to-face human conversation. Drawing on many interviews and a career of writing about communication technology, some of it spent focusing on the benefits of the digital world, Turkle shifts her attention to how smartphones and other digital devices get in the way of developing a complete personality. Few people have put it better: "The new mediated life has gotten us into trouble. Face-to-face conversation is the most human − and humanizing − thing we do. Fully present to one another, we learn to listen. It's where we develop the capacity for empathy. It's where we experience the joy of being heard, of being understood. And conversation advances self-reflection, the conversations with ourselves that are the cornerstone of early development and continue throughout life."[42] Empathy or the ability to put ourselves in the place of others in order to understand them is critical to self- and social development and a life full of screen-mediated experiences makes genuine empathy practically impossible. Turkle argues for cutting back on screen time and spending more in conversations with others and in learning how to reflect on ourselves in unmediated ways. This is undoubtedly valuable advice and few scholars are better than Turkle at delivering what may represent the best revenge of analog. However, it is not easy to translate this into a general social strategy. Short of limiting screen time in schools or incorporating education on how to reclaim conversation in school curricula, both much-needed reforms, it is hard to make what is called "the distracted classroom" part of a political movement. As one approach to taking on the problems that arise in a digital world, reclaiming conversation is important, but limited.

THE VALUE OF IMPOSSIBLE DREAMS

Hard as it is to envision a path forward for the digital world, that may have more to do with a failure of the collective imagination than with a shortage of paths forward. There is a tendency to widespread historical amnesia when it comes to recalling significant progressive social change, especially the speed with which this often occurs. As Mark and Paul Engler remind in their perceptive analysis of social movements "If there is a common trait in the most prominent movements of the past century — whether they involved efforts to end child labor, redefine the role of women in political life, or bring down an apartheid regime — it is that they took up causes that established powerbrokers regarded as sure losers, and won them by creating possibilities that had not previously existed. As the pillars give way, barriers long seen as too daunting to be overcome suddenly appear surmountable."[43]

In the twenty-first century, the example of same-sex marriage stands out as a prime example. When the issue arose in the 1990s legal marriage for same-sex couples was considered an impossible dream. Most did not just oppose it, they considered it to be repugnant. After all, in 1996 President Bill Clinton signed the Defense of Marriage Act, which defined marriage as a union between a man and a woman and denied both recognition and federal benefits to same-sex couples. This came after the U.S. Senate voted to pass the measure by an 85—14 vote. Less than two decades later the Supreme Court ruled that same-sex unions were legal in all 50 states. The Court's decision was just the last event in a long series that began with social movements that used all the tools of political protest, pursued all legal avenues and refused to yield to the dominant view that they were defending a lost cause. Over that relatively short time, public opinion changed from single digits in favor of same-sex unions to majority support. Politicians who declared their opposition through the first decade of the new century, including Hilary Clinton, Joe Biden and Barack Obama, ultimately came to embrace the sudden sea change. None of this would likely have been possible without the firm commitment that activists made to hold fast to an alternative vision about what is possible. We need that commitment today when it comes to creating the Next Internet. Specifically, we need a vision that supports democracy, public control and citizenship over one that promotes elite rule, the acceleration of commercialism, surveillance and militarism. We need to start by addressing users as human beings and digital citizens rather than as consumers and data points.

HISTORICAL IMAGINATION

In addition to this vision, we need to recapture a sense of the history of communication because it provides models that enabled seemingly impossible dreams to be realized in earlier communication systems. This includes recognizing that even before the Founders met to write the Declaration of Independence, they established a nationalized communication system by creating the United States Postal Service. With the Post Office as precedent, nationalization was on the table in debates about subsequent communication technologies. However, owing to a variety of primarily corporate pressures, it was no longer the model of choice. Yet, all subsequent communication systems had to abide by various forms of state intervention.

After the consolidation of early regional telegraph companies, a process that took place between the 1830s and 1860, Western Union became a de facto private monopoly in the United States. While technology permitted continuous drops in prices over that time, the company still pocketed monopoly profits of 30–40 cents on the dollar. As a result, serious attempts were made throughout the period to regulate the company and to break it up. Although some regulations succeeded, most were defeated by the telegraph lobby. Nevertheless, the trade unions and social movement organizations that led the fight learned important lessons that proved useful in the battle against the emerging telephone monopoly led by AT&T.

As a successful and entrenched monopoly, Western Union refused to accept the inevitability of electronic voice communication and turned down opportunities to extend its monopoly, passing on an offer to buy Bell's telephone patents for $100,000. Instead, AT&T grew on its own and did so well that it eventually bought Western Union in 1909, making the telegraph company a key piece of its burgeoning monopoly. This time, however, a communication monopoly was not permitted to operate without restriction. In fact, there were loud calls to nationalize the telephone giant, and, in the face of these, the company agreed to give up its Western Union subsidiary. One reason was the precedent setting case brought by the Justice Department in 1911 that succeeded in using the Sherman Antitrust Act to break up Standard Oil's monopoly in the energy industry. To forestall similar action, AT&T agreed to give up Western Union and permit other telephone companies to interconnect with its system. Two decades later, in the midst of the Great Depression, the U.S. government created the Federal Communication Commission whose job it was to regulate the telecommunications and broadcasting industries "in the public interest, convenience and necessity."

It specifically enshrined a version of the general social compact that protected big companies from what was considered destructive competition and, in return, protected consumers and the full-time, secure jobs of workers in the industry. AT&T was permitted regulated monopoly status and, in return, guaranteed service to all Americans at affordable rates and maintained the unionized jobs of its large workforce. The nationalization model that formed the U.S. Postal Service was set aside in favor of market-based regulation. In 1984, feeling pressure from organizations representing large and small consumers, the government once again intervened, this time to break up AT&T into several smaller companies in the hopes of stimulating competition and innovation.

Almost from its beginning the broadcasting industry was subjected to regulation, antitrust intervention, content regulation of programming and advertising and the requirement to defend its obligation to serve the public interest. Subject to the oversight of first the Federal Radio Commission (1927) and then the Federal Communication Commission (1933), as well as the Federal Trade Commission, and the Department of Justice, the broadcasting system was generally viewed, even as it grew more and more commercial, as a public trust. Indeed, the medium was considered so powerful and the requirement to serve citizens so important that public radio and television networks were established to insure that trust. When new forms of broadcasting such as cable television appeared, these too were subjected to government regulation and oversight.

The computer industry was able to avoid regulation but not without three decades worth of FCC hearings that began in the 1960s to determine how to address the convergence of companies in the unregulated data-processing industry and the regulated telecommunications industry. Given the mounting pressure to free the U.S. computer industry to serve the interests of business, including the defense industry, and the U.S. military and intelligence agencies, the government was not eager to impose regulation. Indeed, the fundamental purpose of the hearings was to keep telecommunications companies, especially AT&T, from throwing their formidable weight around in the emerging sector. Even when it was trying to avoid regulating a new industry, state intervention was required to accomplish this. It turned out that the big threat to an open and competitive computer industry did not come from the telecommunications sector. Rather, it originated from within the computer industry itself and specifically from Microsoft, which threatened to use its dominance over the major operating system and over business software to control the burgeoning online world.

Microsoft recognized early on that software, not hardware, was the ticket to industry power, and achieved it in the pre-Internet days by making its operating systems, first MS-DOS and then Windows, essential for running computer systems. The critical point came in 1981 when IBM, thinking hardware, agreed to sell its operating system to Microsoft and license the subsequent Microsoft-controlled operating system and its upgrades for IBM devices. This made Microsoft the de facto standard for personal computers built by almost all manufacturers. Bill Gates' company used this leverage to secure good terms from the hardware industry and this extended to the Windows OS. Microsoft then used this control to insure that its office tools, including word processing, spread sheet and presentation software, were loaded onto new PCs. Companies that refused to do so were threatened with business-killing retaliation that would deny these companies access to the software that most computers used — all except those running software on then-beleaguered Apple computers.

Fearing that this would make the growth of the information economy, including the military-intelligence sector, utterly dependent on a monopoly, the federal government began to monitor the company in the early 1990s. Closing in on legal action, the Clinton Administration reached a deal in 1994 that allowed Microsoft to keep its operating system monopoly and add new features. However, Gates' firm agreed not to tie new products to Windows. Feeling threatened by the Internet and the growing power of the Netscape web browser, Microsoft stretched the definition of a "feature" to include its own Internet Explorer web browser, which it linked to Windows. Buying a new Windows-based computer, which represented 97 percent of the PC market in 2000, almost always meant a computer that came with Internet Explorer on the desktop. Clearly seeing Explorer as a new product excluded by its deal with the company, the government sued Microsoft on antitrust grounds and, facing the prospect of an AT&T-like breakup, Microsoft settled with the Final Decree taking effect in 2002.

The upshot of all the legal wrangling that resulted was that the company would no longer link Explorer to Windows but reserved the right to do so for future products. What is especially interesting about the case is that many in the Justice Department and in several of the states that joined the suit were very dissatisfied with the agreement, arguing that nothing short of a breakup of the company was warranted. It is certainly arguable that Amazon's current monopoly over key sectors of the online economy meets or exceeds that of Microsoft at the turn of this century, but there has been nothing approaching the government's response to Microsoft. To the contrary, Amazon, and its fellow monopolists comprising the five dominant tech companies, are treated instead as economic saviors. The only government action of any consequence since the Microsoft settlement was the FCC's decision, supported by the Obama Administration, to enact network neutrality, the principle that Internet service providers like Comcast and Time-Warner must permit access to all content and applications regardless of the source, and, what is most important, without favoring or blocking particular products or websites. It prevents Internet service providers from coercing fees from content providers to create pay-to-play fast lanes. The big companies that offer Internet service are in a position to favor their own content sources and block or slow down the sites that feature their competitors or content they do not like. Enacted in 2015, net neutrality would limit their ability to do this. While a significant step forward in creating a more equitable Internet, the decision on Net Neutrality did little to affect the Big Five, which tended to support the principle because it enabled greater openness and equality of access to a network that they dominate. Nevertheless, the principle has spread to other nations in North America, Europe, Latin America and Asia, and provides a unifying thread for social movements fighting for more democratic communication systems.

This brief historical review demonstrates several important points about the potential to take action on the serious issues that are emerging as we enter the Next Internet. First, although it is not often described as such, the very first mass communication system in the United States was a public utility, the U.S. Postal Service. It was created as a government owned and operated communication service available to all. While it is understandable to doubt the likelihood of a public utility on the horizon of the digital world, it is useful to remind ourselves that at a time when the country was more wilderness than society, one of the first acts of its creators was a nationalized public utility in communication. Moreover, the establishment of Post Offices was written into the U.S. Constitutions as an essential government function. Since its creation in 1775 and in spite of inadequate resources and constant ridicule by those who saw this most American of institutions as an aberration from the country's capitalist roots, the USPS served the country well. It provided an essential and universal service, employed millions in good jobs and brought people together across a vast terrain. Modeled after postal systems in Europe and the United Kingdom, it would in turn become a model for many nations whose postal systems arrived later. Although the U.S. and other postal systems have been subjected to various forms of privatization, they remain less commercial than the Internet. It is the Internet not the postal service that routinely accompanies our messages with commercial advertising based on scanning the content of our e-mail and posts to social media sites. All that is keeping us from using the postal service public utility model for the Next Internet is the failure of our public imagination and the pressures of business to make communication serve profit over people. Had Martin Luther King approached civil rights with the same shriveled imagination we bring to the need for democratic communication, we would likely still be drinking from segregated water fountains.

OCCUPY THE INTERNET?

The progress achieved in advancing public communication generally required substantial public intervention that took two general forms. The first involved *structural movements* that aimed to make fundamental changes in American society to expand democracy and equality. These included organized labor, civil rights, consumer protection, public education and other mass movements, which came to see a democratic communication system as an important element to achieve social transformation. These worked with media reform movements that have been an enduring feature of the U.S. communication landscape including near constant struggles to maintain the public postal service, to fight monopoly at Western Union, and then at AT&T, to oppose commercialism in radio, and then television, and now to fight for a free and open Internet. Second, *transactional movement*s worked at the policy- and decision-making levels to put pressure on governments and especially on regulators to change specific laws and regulations. These groups tend to set aside broader structural concerns in order to fight for specific goals like ensuring a social safety net for those who cannot afford telephone or Internet service, resisting government proposals to expand surveillance online, putting pressure on regulators to limit broadcast advertising, especially when it is directed at children, and, most recently, fighting to win the 2015 FCC vote to enact network neutrality. The latter came after a full decade of activism that helped to mobilize nearly 4 million public comments to the FCC.

The distinction between structural and transactional movements is well established in the work of scholar activists like Frances Fox Piven and Jane Jacobs. Piven argued that social movements needed to attack large structural issues such as inequality and poverty. The goal, in her view, was to build national organizations that mobilized mass disruptions to create crises in established systems of exploitation. The National Welfare Rights Organization in the United States represented a model movement that helped to crack open a system that, in the name of eliminating poverty, instead entrenched it more deeply in American society. Jacobs is best known as an activist for communities and cities. Her *Death and Life of Great American Cities* is a model for transactional movements that work from the grass roots to pressure government bodies on specific issues that can make a big difference for cities. For example, a resident of Greenwich

Village in New York City, Jacobs mobilized local community organizations to pressure government bodies, largely controlled by Robert Moses, the city planner and "master builder" who transformed the Greater New York metropolitan area. Moses was finally stopped by community activists, led by Jacobs, when he proposed to construct a major highway across lower Manhattan that would have cut through and decimated historic neighborhoods, including Jacobs' own Greenwich Village, as well as Little Italy and SoHo.

In order to advance citizen control over the Next Internet, we need a combination of Piven's and Jacobs' ideas, including broad structural movements like Occupy Wall Street and offshoots like Occupy the Media and Occupy the FCC. These would use protest and civil disobedience to disrupt the system enough to forcefully demonstrate that the human right to communicate is being trampled in the name of profit. But we also need the transactional work of specialists, including lawyers, economists and other experts who will make the case before the FCC and in the courts. Nowhere did this prove more effective than in opposition to the Trump Administration's Muslim travel ban when millions took to the streets in protest and lawyers and immigration specialists hurried to airports to provide counsel to people turned away from the United States. Making this work in the digital world will require extensive planning. Successful resistance and effective uprisings may appear to occur spontaneously but that is almost never the case.

The big movements of our time including civil rights, feminism, climate change and even the Tea Party, were built on careful development of an overall strategy, specific tactics and backup plans. All of these are required to achieve what today might appear to be the near impossible vision of a democratic digital world. Thankfully there are organizations committed to this struggle, including structural movements like

MoveOn.org and transactional organizations like Free Press. Groups fighting for justice online are springing up all the time. For example, to address the growing problem of embedding racism and sexism in computer algorithms, a graduate researcher at the MIT Media Lab founded the Algorithmic Justice League. The group got started when its founder Joy Buolamwini learned that the software providing robots with facial recognition capabilities more easily identified white faces than they did her black face. Living and working in a world full of robotic devices will be challenging enough without replicating the divisions that afflict the analog world. Groups like this will be essential to free the digital world from automated decision-making based on racist and sexist principles.

The question often arises about the use of online tools to bring about social change. In the early days of their development, much is always made about the power of communication technologies to create social transformation and even revolution. Most of the promise tends to be little more than contributions to the myth-making process that generally succeeds only in promoting the technologies and the corporations that produce them. This century's tools are no exception, the most prominent being the promise that social media would bring democratic revolutions to the Middle East in the so-called Arab Spring. After early success in Tunisia, uprisings spread to Libya, Egypt, Yemen, Syria and Iraq, where modest victories led to massive repression and the return of authoritarian regimes. Social media or no social media, revolution was quashed, just as it was in 1956 when another medium, this time the overseas radio channels of the U.S. government, encouraged the Hungarian people to rise up in rebellion, only to have the Soviet Union bring their courageous struggle to a violent end. We have learned that there is nothing special about communication technologies when it comes to advancing democratic upheavals. Sometimes they contribute; other times they fail, most tragically when, as in the case of Hungary, they provide people with enough false hope to risk their lives in a desperate cause. Communication tools are dynamic in that they can succeed or fail, can often produce unintended consequences, and, a point that is often strangely ignored, can be used effectively by both the powerless and the powerful.

A case in point is cryptocurrency, whose best example is bitcoin, which promises greater freedom from government and corporate controls over standard currencies because cryptocurrency is based on decentralized and distributed tracking of currency movements. In essence, bitcoin and its cousins are promoted as ways to store and spend money without the government or any other authorities knowing about it. Libertarians tend to favor bitcoin because they feel it breaks the shackles of government authority. There is something to be said for keeping the prying eyes of big institutions out of our financial lives, although law-enforcement officials worry that cryptocurrencies represent yet another opportunity to hide illegal transactions. More important, however, is the growing recognition that bitcoin is just as likely to result in advancing the concentration of power and in promoting authoritarian solutions. The key to a successful bitcoin operation is tracking transactions through a distributed "ledger" called a blockchain. Bitcoin owners are cooperatively responsible for overseeing this "mining" process. The problem is that the more bitcoin in circulation, the more is the computing power needed to manage the system. This would require more capital to build, run and maintain the machines, boosting infrastructure and energy costs that could only be borne by large users. Already, two large bitcoin owners in China control about half the mining of the cryptocurrency and, should they join together, could conceivably manipulate the system. Centralization of systems like this is practically inevitable. So if you are hoping to keep the authorities from tracking your whereabouts because you use bitcoin stored on your smartphone to pay for parking, think again. The same technology that liberates you from cash may also drain your bank account and turn off your car when you lack the bitcoin to park it. Or as the neon artist Patrick Martinez puts it in one of his purple-lit creations, "CURRENCY MEANS NOTHIN' IF YOU STILL AIN'T FREE."

More important than the technologies are the people, their planning and their ability to make the right strategic decisions about the choice to pursue structural or transactional movements. For example, if the focus of the Internet of Things industry were directed from profit to people, we would stand a greater chance of developing systems to monitor the climate and advance the safety and efficiency of urban transportation systems. Consider ocean science alone where the Next Internet could sharpen the monitoring of ocean acidification levels to keep closer track of the health of reef ecosystems, changes in sea levels and temperature changes.

It is also important to build on social movements around the world that make extensive use of digital means to advance democracy. Some of the best examples come from Iceland where the Better Reykjavik project crowdsources citizens for civic improvement, and the Pirate party, a substantial force in the nation's Parliament, has its members choose policies in digital and other fora. Similar programs are at work in Brazil (LabHacker), Taiwan (vTaiwan) and in France (Parlement et Citoyens). The MacArthur Foundation in the United States funds a research network that examines how to use digital technologies to involve citizens in the decision-making process and bring more transparency into government. Similar efforts to promote representative democracy are taking place in the United Kingdom through the Open

Governance Research Exchange. In 2017 Jimmy Wales, the founder of Wikipedia, launched the Wikitribune, a crowd-funded site that pays professional journalists to write global news stories and brings in volunteers to vet questionable stories that circulate widely.

BREAK UP THE BIG FIVE

Strong social movements of all sorts are needed because the problems are enormous. Structural and transactional interventions will be essential to address the concentration of power in the Big Five private monopolies. Their power boils down to two fundamental issues, the concentration of power and the commercialism that this power enables. The first requires assertive antitrust action to break up the industry giants. That is because, as Brian Bergstein recognizes, "the problem is not that we need a slightly better Facebook. It's that Facebook — a company worth $400 billion because it vacuums up information about our tastes, our shopping habits, our political beliefs, and just about anything else you might think of — is too powerful in the first place."[44]

It was government antitrust action that forced General Electric to sell the radio giant RCA in 1930. In 1941, it was government action that made RCA divest one of its two radio networks. In 1984 it was government action that succeeded in ending the AT&T monopoly. Today, we need government action to break up one or more of Apple, Google, Amazon, Microsoft and Facebook in order to expand alternative forms of global, national and local communication. At the very least, these companies need to be prevented from using their monopoly power to fend off competition. In the past, RCA and AT&T were granted some leeway because they were viewed as "chosen instruments" or strategic levers for projecting U.S. power and protecting national security. Providing them with some forms of monopoly power was considered in the public interest. Yet, both had to face strong antitrust action. None of today's giants fit the bill of "chosen instrument." In fact, they have made an art of U.S. tax avoidance, choosing overseas tax havens to locate their substantial profits. Moreover, their supply chains primarily make great use of labor outside the United States. In addition, like monopolists throughout history, they stifle innovation. The newspaper industry has lost half of its employees between 2001 and 2016. Billions of dollars have moved from creative companies to Google and others who aggregate news produced by others in order to secure monopoly rents. Nevertheless, as one commentator wrote, "the Justice Department's aggressive antitrust fight with Microsoft nearly two decades ago and even its attempt to block the software company Oracle's acquisition of a rival several years later seem like relics of a forgotten era for the tech industry in the United States."[45] At the very least, the Big Five should be prohibited from buying new companies. Google's purchase of online ad giant DoubleClick and Facebook's deal for Instagram exemplify how today's monopolies get built. This must be stopped. It would also be useful to remove the "safe harbor" provision of the 1998 Digital Millennium Copyright Act, which protects platform companies from being held responsible for their content. The provision gives Facebook and others the incentive to host the most offensive material as long as they can attract advertising.

Societies should also begin to experiment with new forms of data ownership. There is no reason, other than sheer corporate power, that the Big Five should own the data that users generate on their networks. In effect these companies get to profit from our posts without accepting any legal responsibility for what is posted. Citizenship should include the right to own and control our own data, which, like phone numbers and other identifiers, we should have the right to move to the networks of our choice. This would provide opportunities for competing platforms, both private and public.

The United States can learn from the European Union, which has taken the first steps in what may constitute a path forward on antitrust action. This includes a $122 million fine levied against Facebook in May 2017 for lying to the EU on its $19 billion purchase of the Internet messaging service WhatsApp in 2014. A condition of EU approval was Facebook's agreement that it would not share customer data with WhatsApp. When the social media giant broke the agreement, the EU acted, something that the U.S. government, whether led by Barack Obama or Donald Trump, has refused to do. Facebook agreed to pay the fine, arguably small by Facebook standards, but the punishment nevertheless broke records for such infractions. In addition, 2017 saw the EU hit Google with a $2.7 billion fine for abusing its monopoly by placing its own comparison shopping site ahead of others in search results. When will the United States act?

REGULATE COMMERCIALISM

Attacking ownership concentration is important, but breaking up the giants must be accompanied by limiting commercialism in the Next Internet. It may appear quaint to recall that radio broadcasters in the 1920s and 1930s were allowed to air commercials only during daytime business hours and only to identify the corporate sponsor of a program. It is now appearing similarly unusual to have once limited the time a television station was permitted set aside for advertising.

Almost all of these rules are now gone and commercialism is both rampant and universal. Companies monetize the most intimate of private communication. Imagine if handwritten letters came with ads tailored to what we know about the wants and needs of the recipient or if our telephone conversations were interspersed with commercials customized to the subject of the call. Libraries and reference volumes that once provided a public alternative to the commercial world have given way to online alternatives where information passes through advertising filters and what remains of legitimate information is presented with pitches for products and services. Fake news is only a small part of what has become a full-blown legitimation crisis in knowledge and communication brought about by the insinuation of advertising into all facets of information production and distribution.

To address the crisis requires a commitment to regulate commercialism, especially in online search and social media. At the very least, Google should not be permitted to give top of the list priority to advertisements connected to search terms. It should be prohibited from giving priority to commercial sites, and similarly forbidden to allow ads on its search pages. Moreover, Facebook should not be permitted to monetize posts by selling the words and images we create to advertisers. Ads on Facebook pages should be severely limited and those that promote hate, violence, racism and sexism need to be banned outright. Facebook needs to be held accountable for what it publishes, just as newspapers and broadcasters have been held accountable in the past. To rescue genuine information and communication from the black hole of commercialism requires strong intervention. It also requires one or more public alternatives to the dominant commercial entities. When commercial media failed the public interest in the past, public radio and television provided genuine alternatives to the commercial singularity.

This was the case even in the United States, when its media arteries clogged with ads. Whether through general tax revenues or taxes on the monopoly rents that Big Tech earns from its lock on advertising dollars and the tools powering the Next Internet, it is essential to devise alternative means of communication that are public, democratic and available to all. The original Internet promised this. It has failed. Now that failure may be compounded in the even more powerful world of the Cloud, Big Data and the Internet of Things, what one business writer warns is now the leading edge of "totalitarian capitalism."[46] He concludes that we must not make the same mistakes that the Clinton and Obama Administrations made in backing off on strong regulation of the tech sector and instead push to strengthen the admittedly weak efforts the EU has made to stand up to a force that is arguably more powerful than the phony "populism" that appears to be sweeping the world.

RESIST MILITARISM

A major reason why it is difficult to diminish the power of Big Tech is that it is closely tied to the military. There is nothing new here. RCA was founded from a deal with the U.S. Navy to consolidate patents so that the United States would be able to fend off challenges from Great Britain. From 1922 to 1930 a high-ranking military officer was President and Chairman of the Board, preceding David Sarnoff who also had close military ties. AT&T was the major provider of telecommunications services to the Department of Defense. Its close ties to the military helped the company keep its monopoly intact for many years. In fact, it was not until the Pentagon assented to the breakup of the company that the deal went through. Today Silicon Valley firms are primary suppliers to the military and intelligence agencies. The friendship between the Valley and the Pentagon is not always cozy. There are times when Big Tech resists demands to expand government surveillance and spying. This tends to happen when companies fear that shining a light on their involvement in the military-information complex will hurt business. Diminishing the deadly power of this system starts precisely with disseminating, as widely as possible, information on the complicity of Big Tech in mass government surveillance, in the expansion of robotic warfare and in the killing power of weaponized drones. It is not just about the concentration of economic power or of commercialism. The Next Internet is also a military force that routinely violates the right to privacy and, ultimately, the right to live free from the threat of a completely militarized world.

The challenge to resist is formidable. Even after all the revelations about illegal NSA spying and even after reforms were instituted, the Agency still managed to collect and process 151 million phone records in 2016. Those who argue that this is a hopeless cause need to recall that ending the U.S. war in Viet Nam was also once considered an impossible dream. War resisters and protesters who joined the uprising against a war that mobilized 500,000 U.S. combat troops, that featured daily bombing raids on civilian populations across the region and that had the support of politicians across America, overcame massive odds to end the war and force the removal of the U.S. presence. Consider that in 1969 the then Governor of California Ronald Reagan announced that "If it takes a bloodbath to silence the demonstrators, let's get it over with" just before police attacked protesters in Berkeley.[47] Facing this and more, the resistance then ended a war. A similar uprising against Big Tech's alliance with the military is needed today.

It is also especially important to begin developing bilateral and multilateral agreements to control the growing danger of cyber warfare. Those who doubt whether such treaties are possible in a digital world need to recall that similar questions were raised about relatively successful nuclear, chemical and biological weapons agreements. Moreover, they need to reflect on the danger of failing to forge a regulatory regime. We now have weapons that can operate quietly and secretly to bring down the global Internet and the vital infrastructure that depends on the digital world to deliver food, water and power to most of the world's people. Alluding to the first use of nuclear weapons on a civilian population, the former head of both the NSA and the CIA, Michael Hayden, powerfully captured the threat of cyber warfare when he told an interviewer in the documentary film Zero Days: "This has the whiff of August, 1945."

CONTROL E-POLLUTION

Action is also urgently needed on the environmental consequences of the Next Internet. This includes shifting from energy guzzling power sources for Cloud data centers, including back-up systems, Internet of Things device sensors and the networks that converging Next Internet systems rely on to transmit incessantly growing data amounts. Lobbies for the coal and oil industries eagerly anticipate major leaps in energy use. These must be resisted. Solar, wind and other renewable and sustainable energy sources are an essential starting point. But the only way this can happen today is through public pressure. There is no organized system in place to require Big Tech or any of the other private tech companies or government agencies to require the rational use of energy for the Next Internet. Nor is there any rational plan in place for locating data centers. U.S. data centers tend to be sited in Northern Virginia, which is proximate to the populous Boston to Washington corridor and in California where Silicon Valley is located. This makes some business sense but little environmental sense. For data centers to minimize cooling requirements it is best to build them in northern locations. That is why Scandinavia and Canada are good choices and some companies have taken advantage of them for this reason and because ample cold water supplies save on the need for air conditioning to cool servers. This makes far more sense than placing them in California where water issues are a fundamental problem and earthquakes are a fact of life. The environmental organization Greenpeace has brought significant attention to these issues, but much more needs to be done to bring them to the public's attention and to mobilize a public response.

We also need mass mobilization to address the issue of e-waste. The problem attracted public attention in the United States in the early years of the personal computer because some manufacturing was still taking place in the United States and the state of California was the home of major waste sites. Attention was also called to the strange cottage industry of semiconductor manufacturing at home in California where poor and undocumented workers risked toxic poisoning to earn a few dollars working for growing companies in the burgeoning tech industry. Waste sites seemed to be everywhere, with many qualifying for special federal Superfund money to clean up the toxic waste. Soon after the issue heated up and began to draw national political attention, companies began to ship both the manufacturing jobs and the e-waste from devices overseas, especially to China. This only shifted the problem to another part of the world. Today there is not much being done to deal with these toxic mountains and little in planning about what to do with the mountains to come.

At the very least, it is essential to inform people that the digital world is far from immaterial and that we need to plan for the safe recycling and disposal of these very material objects and the rare metals and toxic chemicals they contain. The massive expansion of devices that is coming with the Next Internet, especially the sensors contained in Internet of Things devices, workplace robots and military equipment, especially weaponized drones, makes this an especially pressing issue. The United Nations World Health Organization has taken a leading role in an international information campaign and in bringing together affected countries, those doing the dumping and those receiving it, in global accords that propose joint action. The WHO has paid special attention to children who are exposed to chemicals from e-waste in their homes. Unsafe recycling techniques, such as burning cables to secure copper, expose children to a range of hazardous substances. Dangerous exposure also results from proximity to dump sites located close to their homes, schools and play areas. The WHO works closely with national environmental organizations to promote proper recycling and disposal, especially the U.S. Environmental Protection Agency. Effective as some of these efforts have been in promoting e-waste safety, the limitations of these essentially transactional approaches to change are becoming increasingly clear. The rise of authoritarian regimes, especially in the United States and United Kingdom, has meant reduced funding and major rollbacks in these programs. In the absence of social movements committed to structural reforms in the production and distribution of digital devices, major progress is unlikely. The work of the Basel Action Network (BAN), along with the research of MIT's Senseable City Lab, are positive steps. They have tracked e-waste supply chains and provided significant assistance to citizen groups putting much-needed pressure on guilty corporations and governments.

RESTORE PRIVACY

Even though problems surrounding privacy and surveillance have been with us for quite some time, it is not easy to mobilize large numbers of people to rise up in support of limiting surveillance and expanding privacy. Admittedly, we have never experienced the breadth of surveillance that is today part of everyday life. Hacking appears to be a daily occurrence. The commercial collection of data about online communications and online transactions is often met with a shrug. In response to the massive expansion of government surveillance, people often support it because they believe constant monitoring contributes to combatting criminal and terrorist threats and because they believe that surveillance is not a problem for those who have done no wrong.

One way to deal with these issues is to turn away from the mistaken but popular belief that privacy is nothing more than a transactional good, all or parts of which we can exchange for convenience, ease of communication and a 24/7 ubiquitous connection. Rather, privacy, like communication, is an essential human right that provides the necessary space for personal development. Privacy advocates, their organizations and movements need to make a convincing case that viewing privacy as a tradable commodity is not like giving up a thing but more like giving up our essential selves. Moreover, advocates must make the case that violations linked to hacking, which receive the lion's share of media attention, are a small part of the privacy picture. Surveillance capitalism, as led by Google, Facebook and their corporate partners in the Next Internet, represents a more significant threat to who we are. Consider that Facebook now makes use of its massive surveillance systems to gather data on Facebook users who are going through a relationship breakup. This is done, the company openly admits, to assist its advertisers by providing them with verified information on how to market products and services that Facebook's analytics research demonstrates people in the midst of a breakup tend to buy. Such violations of the self constitute a form of abuse that must be stopped with strengthened privacy legislation and a movement of people committed to stopping the abuse. At the very least, we need to ban unreadable privacy agreements in favor of clear ones that detail the extent of privacy violations that follow from any agreement to participate in social media such as online shopping. Moreover, we need to require that companies provide explicit statements about how customer data will be used and receive active consent before doing so. Also, such consent needs to be reviewed on a regular basis. Privacy is too important to be given up once and have that decision live on forever.

There is far more online government surveillance than is necessary to deal with criminal activity. It has taken the work of courageous whistle blowers like Edward Snowden to teach the world just how excessive is government surveillance. Organizations like the National Security Agency gather growing amounts of intelligence because the technology enables it and because the surveillance state is committed to controlling its own citizens and those in other countries. Snowden revealed the extent of the NSA's surveillance and the willing cooperation of corporations keen to curry favor with a government that supports their economic power and tolerates their ability to shelter profits abroad. Indeed the collusion between the surveillance state and surveillance capitalism is arguably the greatest threat posed by the Next Internet.

Organizations like the American Civil Liberties Union and the Electronic Frontier Foundation in the United States have made significant contributions to the fight against unbridled surveillance. Their counterparts abroad, including social movements and political organizations, like Pirate Parties

International, which represents members in over 40 nations, have been successful in raising consciousness about surveillance. They have also succeeded in pressuring representative institutions, like the European Union, to take a tougher stance on the issue. The EU has been more active than the US government, including determining that Facebook violated the EU's own modest data privacy rules. Soon after the EU levied one of the most substantial fines in Facebook's history for sharing customer data in connection with its purchase of WhatsApp, the privacy watchdogs of the Netherlands and France decided that Facebook was guilty of breaking data-protection laws. It is also notable that Germany is getting tough with social media companies, including levying major penalties for failures to police hate speech and for spreading misinformation. Nevertheless, policy remedies can have unwanted consequences outside the privacy arena. For example, by imposing blanket restrictions on the use of cookies in order to protect privacy, EU regulators will likely give Facebook and Google greater control over the digital marketplace because the restrictions limit publishers' ability to attract essential advertising revenue. The Next Internet, and especially the Internet of Things, raises the stakes for privacy and surveillance, making it more essential than ever to take action if we are to restore and strengthen the human right to privacy.

BASIC INCOME IS A HUMAN RIGHT

Automation is beginning to have a profound impact in the workplace. Over the 40 years I have been writing about communication technology, each wave of new technologies brought predictions about job loss that were not realized. As it turns out, the primary shift in global labor over the past

50 years has been the massive movement of industrial jobs from the West to China, some of which have been replaced with lower paying service and retail work. As a result the West has experienced pockets of decline in its industrial heartland alongside the equally significant growth of service occupations. The transformation has been undoubtedly significant, not the least because it contributed to political upheavals such as Brexit, the election of Donald Trump and the growing worldwide popularity of authoritarian regimes. The primary reasons for the transformation are social, political and economic, not technological. They arise from trade agreements that offered the West low-wage industrial labor from less developed countries and, in return, China, India and other Asian nations received a path to rapid development. However, with the growth of the Next Internet, forecasts of automation-induced unemployment may finally be realized.

The replacement of living with dead labor has always promised significant cost savings but could not be easily realized until dead labor was given enough artificial intelligence or decision-making capabilities to carry out the jobs of skilled and semiskilled labor, not just the work performed by unskilled laborers. The convergence of the Cloud with Big Data and the Internet of Things means that the time has arrived when executives in the financial services industry are joining telephone operators and factory workers in the ranks of the unemployed. This does not mean that all jobs are at risk, nor does it mean that all at-risk jobs will disappear. But research suggests that half *are* at risk, and given the cost savings, many, if not most of these, will fade away as career paths for human workers. One study by the Obama White House forecasts that 83 percent of workers earning under $20 per hour would lose their jobs. Moreover, many skilled and unskilled workers are right now in the process of training their automated replacements.

The declining cost and miniaturization of the sensors and processors that comprise artificial intelligence devices make them increasingly cost-effective, even for the lowest-wage countries. As a result, even China, where the world's factories once found seemingly unlimited cheap labor, is deploying robotics throughout the workforce. This results from labor shortages in China owing to its one-child policy, the lack of interest in factory labor among China's increasingly prosperous population and the growing ability of China's blue-collar workforce to command higher wages.

There are increasing calls for action across the political spectrum to address this likely structural shift in the production and distribution of goods and services. These typically start with proposals for more education and training with specific attention to those skills that are unlikely to be automated or at least those jobs for which human labor is likely to retain the upper hand over machines. In a nod to the need for training in analog skills, jobs requiring strong face-to-face communication skills, whether with customers, fellow workers, suppliers or investors, are attracting special attention. There is also a great need for training in human–machine communication, an area that has been understandably ignored because there were few machines that required more than occasional programming, maintenance and upgrading. Intelligent machines are increasingly the workmates of human employees who will have to learn unique interactive skills to maintain a reasonably harmonious relationship. In the past, when machines broke down, we used to joke that they had minds of their own. They now do.

Because neo-liberalism stripped most of the power that trade unions once wielded, workers have little recourse and practically no say in the radical transformation underway.

There have been some legislative attempts to provide a basic package of benefits to the millions of gig economy workers who lack the ability to take sick days, protect themselves from the economic impact of a sudden disability or make even the most minimal investment toward their retirement. None of these efforts have succeeded in the United States. However, unions representing creative employees have made it easier for workers to deal with the inevitable ups and downs of the industry. For example, when the online news platform Huffington Post laid off scores of workers in 2017, 39 were represented by the Writers Guild of America East and were protected by a union contract that provided severance pay and ongoing health benefits. Moreover, there are grounds for hope in the European Union, and especially Germany, where unions retain enough power to threaten even dominant Big Tech firms such as Amazon whose attempts to apply American-style management, with its bare bones pay packages and no benefits, have been rebuffed by organized labor.

In the absence of a major reversal in labor—management relations, the primary policy response that might prove beneficial for the mass of citizens is a guaranteed basic income provided to all as a right of citizenship. There are many different plans and a variety of names given to the concept. The essential idea has been around for some time, at least as early as the 1970s when the Nixon Administration considered a basic income plan. Francis Piven, who provided intellectual and political leadership to social movements for structural reform, was an early force as well. She hoped that by overloading the traditional social welfare system, with its repressive bureaucracy, means tests and surveillance, the system would collapse and be replaced by some form of universal income.

Basic income proposals derive from the recognition that the onrush of automation will leave many without the likelihood of finding a job that pays a living wage. Such a situation will not only increase poverty. It also has the potential to diminish demand significantly enough to put economies in a constant state of stagnation that risks regular downward spirals into recession and depression. The idea of a universal basic income has attracted considerable international attention, with Finland, Canada, the Netherlands and Italy all involved in a range of national and local trials. Traditional promoters of free market capitalism provide formidable opposition, but many business leaders are backing the idea. This includes leaders in the tech community, such as Facebook founder Mark Zuckerberg and Sam Altman, president of the powerful venture capital firm Y Combinator. Moreover, the growing recognition that accelerating inequality is an urgent problem has mobilized social movements that view universal income proposals as the leading edge of a progressive offensive in a post-Internet world. The pressure of social movements will be particularly important when the idea reaches the point of producing detailed policies because the actual significance of a universal basic income will be determined by the amounts of funding and the eligibility requirements. How universal? How basic? What, if any, are the employment requirements?

CONCLUSION: TOWARDS A PUBLIC UTILITY IN COMMUNICATION

In 1775, America's founders established a public utility in communication, the United States Postal Service and in 1787 made it part of the original Constitution. They recognized the need for a universal system of communication that was public, open and accessible. This achievement receives precious little attention because it clashes with the capitalist principles that steered the country's development and it butts heads with the myth that America's founders believed that communication systems should be free from government intervention. These views and similar vilifications have served the interests of those driven by the need to fight against any public institutions that might cut into their profit potential. Nevertheless, when the telegraph, telephone, broadcasting and the Internet arrived, the principles of America's first public utility, including universality, equality and open communication provided a foundation for resistance to fully commercial systems. Moreover, the United States built on this foundation by creating repositories for knowledge in the Library of Congress and a national network of public libraries. It also created public universities to extend that knowledge through publicly funded research that has proven invaluable to citizens and to business. These were created amidst battles for control over the communication system that specifically addressed ownership concentration, public interest regulation, excessive commercialism, network neutrality and numerous others that shaped the contested terrain of communication technology history. As we enter the Next Internet, it is important to keep both the principles and the battles in mind. It is time to once again consider the need for a public utility in communication.

The concept of a public utility in computer communication is not new. In fact, the idea was seriously discussed well before the first personal computer. In 1966, a Canadian researcher working for the federal Department of Communication wrote *The Challenge of the Computer Utility*, describing how to bring the power of information technology to everyone. In this work Douglas Parkhill foresaw the arrival of Cloud Computing and envisioned the link between this form of information storage and provision and the public utility form of resource management that had worked for water and power. Recognizing that information is neither electricity nor water, he nevertheless understood that there were enough similarities to warrant comparisons between information and other essential services. Parkhill foresaw centralized storage in large data centers but he also expected flexibility in management and organization because information utilities could be provided on public or regulated private bases and located at the community, national or even global level.

Parkhill's ideas are similar to those introduced at around the same time by computer pioneers in the United States including J. C. R. Licklider who was a primary source behind the Arpanet, the Department of Defense's precursor to the Internet. Licklider's work on time-sharing computers anticipated the Cloud and his vision of a universal system, or what he called the Intergalactic Computer Network, made up of a handful of computers provisioning the nation with data and software resembles Parkhill's utility concept. So too do those of John McCarthy, another computer pioneer, who imagined public utility networks built on the model of computer service bureaus that provided centralized IT services for subscribing customers. These ideas were sequestered when the personal computer and local storage arrived, but they have returned with the Cloud and all the problems associated with a fully commercial system.

Today, the vision of a democratic post-Internet world has motivated social movements like Free Press in the United States to mobilize in support of network neutrality, which guarantees equal access to the networks moving data along the Internet. There is debate on its significance but net neutrality would undoubtedly take a step on the way to making the Internet a public utility. Its significance is not lost on the Trump Administration, which began to dismantle net neutrality regulations within five months of taking office. Meanwhile, other governments and major political parties have adopted policies that make progress towards the public utility model. The government of Canada has formally adopted net neutrality provisions and is considering proposals to rein in the power of Big Tech. The UK Labor Party has adopted a Digital Manifesto that proposes far-reaching measures to support broadening universal access, greater openness, public platform cooperatives to counter the power of major tech and social media companies, open source software to address the stranglehold of corporate control over intellectual property and other measures that would broaden citizen power in the post-Internet world.

As the IT industry increasingly recognizes, the information utility concept is a technical extension of Cloud Computing because it centralizes data, software, applications and services in the Cloud. Concentrating the power to carry out this process in a handful of dominant companies led by Amazon, Google and Facebook has created many problems. At the very least, their ability to enhance monopoly through mergers and acquisitions must be stopped and their safe harbor from taking responsibility for content posted to their platforms must be ended. Indeed, in addition to creating genuine public information utilities, we should seriously consider regulating the Big Five as public utilities by requiring them to license out patents for search algorithms, advertising exchanges and other key innovations for a nominal fee. Moreover, it is time to rethink a system that concentrates control over data in a handful of companies primarily interested in using data for profit. Public utilities would keep public data under citizen control. The decision to use data for public benefit should be made by citizens and their representatives whether that means providing it to public institutions such as schools and health authorities or licensing it to private entities, which would pay for the right to create platforms that draw from data.

Building public information utilities offers an alternative to the singular dominance of the Big Five and their equally singular commitment to commodifying and militarizing the entire production, distribution and use of data, information, knowledge and entertainment. Public information utilities would be driven by the commitment to universal and equal access to open networks. They would support public control over platforms for social media to create a genuine electronic commons. They would also promote analog alternatives to the digital world. Moreover, public information utilities would provide an essential space for addressing the environmental, privacy and workplace issues that bedevil the post-Internet world. We now have the technical capacity to achieve these goals. It remains to be seen whether we can build the social movements essential to bringing about a more democratic and egalitarian post-Internet world.

ENDNOTES

[1]Mell, P., & Grance, T. (2009). *The NIST definition of cloud computing*. Washington, DC: National Institute of Standards and Technology. Retrieved from https://www.nist.gov/sites/-default/files/documents/itl/cloud/cloud-def-v15.pdf. Accessed on July 8, 2017.

[2]Anderson, C. (2008). The end of theory: The data deluge makes the scientific method obsolete. *Wired*, June 23. Retrieved from www.wired.com/2008/06/pb-theory. Accessed on June 1, 2017.

[3]Martin, T. W., & Jeong, E.-Y. (2017). In the chips: Tech's sleeping giant becomes a $352 Billion cash cow. *The Wall Street Journal*, April 26. Retrieved from https://www.wsj.com/articles/chips-ahoy-techs-sleeping-giant-becomes-a-352-billion-cash-cow-1493217440. Accessed on June 12, 2017.

[4]U.S. Government, Subcommittee on Networking and Information Technology Research and Development. (2016, May). *Federal big data research and development strategic plan* (p. 1). Washington, DC. Retrieved from https://www.nitrd.gov/PUBS/bigdatardstrategicplan.pdf. Accessed on June 15, 2017.

[5]U.S. Government, The Department of Commerce Internet Policy Task Force & Digital Economy Leadership Team. (2017, January). *Fostering the advancement of the internet of*

things (p. 1). Washington, DC. Retrieved from https://www. ntia.doc.gov/files/ntia/publications/iot_green_paper_01122017. pdf. Accessed on June 15, 2017.

[6]Harris, K. (2015). Killer robots pose risks and advantages for military use. *CBC News*, April 10. Retrieved from http:// www.cbc.ca/m/touch/politics/story/1.3026963. Accessed on June 15, 2017.

[7]Bradsher, K. (2016). When solar panels become job killers. *The New York Times*, April 8. Retrieved from https:// www.nytimes.com/2017/04/08/business/china-trade-solar-panels.html?_r=0. Accessed on June 15, 2017.

[8]Daod, E. (2016). Control your mobile through the Duoskin 'Smart' Tatoo. *news.com.au*, August 18. Retrieved from http://www.news.com.au/technology/innovation/control-your-mobile-through-the-duoskin-smart-tattoo/news-story/5588c792f1754d0d2d5b973b16342d03. Accessed on June 15, 2017.

[9]Payne, S. (2015). Stockholm: Members of epicenter workspace are using microchip implants to open doors. *International Business Times*, January 31. Retrieved from http://www.ibtimes.co.uk/stockholm-office-workers-epicenter-implanted-microchips-pay-their-lunch-1486045. Accessed on June 16, 2017.

[10]*Ibid.*

[11] Solon, O. (2017). Facebook is hiring moderators: But is the job too difficult for humans? *The Guardian*, May 4. Retrieved from www.theguardian.com/technology/2017/may/04/facebook-content-moderators-ptsd-psychological-dangers. Accessed on June 18, 2017.

[12]Menegus, B. (2016). Lyft thinks it's 'exciting' that a driver was working while giving birth. *Gizmodo*, September 22. Retrieved from www.gizmodo.com/lyft-thinks-its-exciting-that-a-driver-was-working-whil-1786970298. Accessed on June 18, 2017.

[13]Tolentino, J. (2017). The gig economy celebrates working yourself to death. *The New Yorker*, March 22. Retrieved from www.newyorker.com/culture/jia-tolentino/the-gig-economy-celebrates-working-yourself-to-death. Accessed on June 18, 2017.

[14]Daugman, J. (1990). Brain metaphor and brain theory. In E. L. Schwartz (Ed.), *Computational neuroscience* (p. 15). Cambridge, MA: MIT Press.

[15]U.S. Government, Defense Advanced Research Projects Agency. (2016). Bridging the bio-electronic divide. Washington, DC: DARPA. Retrieved from www.darpa.mil/news-events/ 2015-01-19. Accessed on June 19, 2017.

[16]Anthony, A. (2017). Yuval Noah Harari: 'Homo sapiens as we know them will disappear in a century or so'. *The Guardian*, March 19. Retrieved from www.theguardian.com/ culture/2017/mar/19/yuval-harari-sapiens-readers-questions-lucy-prebble-arianna-huffington-future-of-humanity. Accessed on June 19, 2017.

[17]O'Gieblyn, M. (2017). God in the machine: My strange journey into transhumanism. *The Guardian*, April 18. Retrieved from www.theguardian.com/technology/2017/apr/ 18/god-in-the-machine-my-strange-journey-into-transhumanism. Accessed on June 19, 2017.

[18]Barnouw, E. (1968). *The golden web* (p. 234). Oxford University Press.

[19]Levin, S. (2017, April 7). Google accused of 'extreme' gender pay discrimination by US Labor Department. *The Guardian*. Retrieved from www.theguardian.com/technology/ 2017/apr/07/google-pay-disparities-women-labor-department-lawsuit. Accessed June 19, 2017.

[20]Naughton, J. (2017, April 23). How Facebook became a home to psychopaths. *The Guardian* , Retrieved from www.theguardian.com/commentisfree/2017/apr/23/how-facebook-

became-home-to-psychopaths-facebook-live. Accessed on June 19, 2017.

[21]Bergen, M. (2017, April 3). Google updates ads policies again, ramps up AI to curtail YouTube crisis. *Bloomberg Technology*. Retrieved from www.bloomberg.com/news/articles/2017-04-03/google-updates-ads-polices-again-ramps-up-ai-to-curtail-youtube-crisis. Accessed on June 19, 2017.

[22]Alba, D. (2017, April 21). The hidden laborers training AI to keep ads off hateful YouTube videos. *Wired*. Retrieved from www.wired.com/2017/04/zerochaos-google-ads-quality-raters/. Accessed on June 19, 2017).

[23]Cadwalladr, C. (2016, December 4). Google, democracy and the truth about Internet search. *The Guardian*. Retrieved from www.theguardian.com/technology/2016/dec/04/google-democracy-truth-internet-search-facebook. Accessed on June 19, 2017.

[24]Greenspon, E., & Owen, T. (2017, May 29). 'Fake News 2.0': A threat to Canada's democracy. *The Globe and Mail*. Retrieved from www.theglobeandmail.com/opinion/fake-news-20-a-threat-to-canadas-democracy/article35138104/. Accessed on June 19, 2017.

[25]Bell, E. & Owen, T. (2017, March 29). *The platform press: How Silicon Valley reengineered journalism*. Report of the Tow Center for Digital Journalism, New York. Retrieved from https://www.cjr.org/tow_center_reports/platform-press-how-silicon-valley-reengineered-journalism.php. Accessed on June 19, 2017.

[26]Gusterson, H. (2015). *Drones: Remote control warfare* (p. 1). Cambridge, MA: MIT Press.

[27]U.S. Government, Department of Commerce (2017, January). *Fostering the advancement of the Internet of Things*, Washington, D.C. p. 10. Retrieved from https://www.ntia.doc.gov/files/ntia/publications/iot_green_paper_01122017.pdf. Accessed on June 20, 2017.

[28]Steckel, J., Edenhofer, O., & Jakob, M. (2015). Drivers for the renaissance of coal. *Proceedings of the National Academy of Science* 112(29), E3775–E3781.

[29]Mills, M.P. (2013). *The cloud begins with coal: big data, big networks, big infrastructure, and big power*. Digital Power Group, p. 3. Retrieved from www.tech-pundit.com/wp-content/uploads/2013/07/Cloud_Begins_With_Coal.pdf. Accessed on June 21, 2017.

[30]Cullinen, M. (2013). *Machine to machine technologies: Unlocking the potential of a $1 trillion industry*. Carbon War Room. Retrieved from http://www.grahampeacedesignmail.com/cwr/cwr_m2m_down_singles.pdf. Accessed on June 21, 2017.

[31]Leach, A. (2016, October 18). The E-waste mountains. *The Guardian*. Retrieved from https://www.theguardian.com/global-development-professionals-network/gallery/2016/oct/18/the-e-waste-reduce-waste-old-technology-mountains-in-pictures. Accessed on June 21, 2017.

[32]Hague, M. (2017, April 18). Stupid homes: Experts suggest people create space without technology. *The Globe and Mail*. Retrieved from https://www.theglobeandmail.com/life/home-and-garden/stupid-homes-experts-suggest-people-create-space-without-technology/article34734653/. Accessed on June 21, 2017.

[33]Powles, J. (2015, July 15). Internet of Things: The greatest mass surveillance infrastructure ever? *The Guardian*. Retrieved from https://www.theguardian.com/technology/2015/jul/15/internet-of-things-mass-surveillance. Accessed on June 21, 2017.

[34]Hadhazy, A. (2017, April 18). Biased bots: Artificial-intelligence systems echo human prejudices. Princeton University. Retrieved from https://www.princeton.edu/news/2017/04/18/biased-bots-artificial-intelligence-systems-echo-human-prejudices. Accessed on June 22, 2017.

[35]Hinchliffe, E. (2017, March 14). Edward Snowden explains exactly how the CIA would hack your Samsung TV. *Mashable*. Retrieved from http://mashable.com/2017/03/14/wikileaks-snowden-interview/#f.Hgb5cIYOqB. Accessed on June 22, 2017.

[36]McKendrick, J. (2013, February 19). In the rush to cloud computing, here's one question not enough people are asking. *Forbes*. Retrieved from https://www.forbes.com/sites/joemckendrick/2013/02/19/in-the-rush-to-cloud-computing-heres-one-question-not-enough-people-are-asking/#4a9a017d7194. Accessed on June 22, 2017.

[37]Dignan, L. (2011, October 24). Cloud computing's real creative destruction may be the IT workforce. *ZDNet*. Retrieved from http://www.zdnet.com/article/cloud-computings-real-creative-destruction-may-be-the-it-workforce/. Accessed on June 22, 2017.

[38]*Ibid.*

[39]Dignan, L. (2011, October 18). Analytics in 40 years: Machines will kick human managers to the curb. *ZDNet*. Retrieved from http://www.zdnet.com/article/analytics-in-40-years-machines-will-kick-human-managers-to-the-curb/. Accessed on June 22, 2017.

[40]See endnote 37.

[41]McKendrick, J. (2014, August 11). We're all outsourcers now, thanks to cloud. *Forbes*. Retrieved from https://www.forbes.com/sites/joemckendrick/2014/08/11/were-all-outsourcers-now-thanks-to-cloud/#2f101e5b67aa. Accessed on June 22, 2017.

[42]Turkle, S. (2015). *Reclaiming conversation: The power of talk in the digital age* (p. 3). New York, NY: Penguin.

[43]Engler, M., & Engler, P. (2016). *This is an uprising* (p. 114). New York, NY: Nation Books.

[44]Bergstein, B. (2017, April 10). We need more alternatives to Facebook. *MIT Technology Review*. Retrieved from

https://www.technologyreview.com/s/604082/we-need-more-alternatives-to-facebook/. Accessed on June 24, 2017.

[45]Kerstetter, J. (2017, May 19). Daily report: Europe gets tough on Facebook. *The New York Times*. Retrieved from https://mobile.nytimes.com/2017/05/19/technology/daily-report-europe-gets-tough-on-facebook.html. Accessed on July 18, 2017.

[46]Mortished, C. (2017, May 14). The totalitarian capitalism of tech giants should trump your fears of populism. *The Globe and Mail*. Retrieved from https://tgam.ca/2s4kazR. Accessed on June 24, 2017.

[47]Simon, M., & Carlsen, W. (2004, June 6). Hard line helped him win, flexibility helped him stay / Ability to compromise replaced his tough stance against UC student protests. *San Francisco Chronicle*. Retrieved from http://www.sfgate.com/news/article/Hard-line-helped-him-win-flexibility-helped-him-2751983.php. Accessed on June 24, 2017.

EPIGRAPH REFERENCES

Schwartz, A. The Art and Activism of Grace Paley. *The New Yorker*, May 8, 2007. Retrieved from http://www.newyorker.com/magazine/2017/05/08/the-art-and-activism-of-grace-paley. Accessed on August 1, 2017.

Williams, R. (2015). *Keywords* (p. xxxv). New York, NY: Oxford University Press.

Le Guin, U. K. (2004). A Rant About 'Technology'. Retrieved from http://www.ursulakleguin.com/Note-Technology.html. Accessed on August 1, 2017.

Mortished, C. The Totalitarian Capitalism of Tech Giants Should Trump Your Fears of Populism. *The Globe and Mail*. Retrieved from https://beta.theglobeandmail.com/report-on-business/economy/economic-insight/the-totalitarian-capitalism-

of-tech-giants-should-trump-your-fears-of-populism/article3498
3932/. Accessed on August 1, 2017.

Shapin, S. (2017, July 13) The Superhuman Upgrade. *The London Review of Books* (Vol. 39, No. 14). Retrieved from https://www.lrb.co.uk/v39/n14/steven-shapin/the-superhuman-upgrade. Accessed on August 1, 2017.

Baumann, Z. (1998). *Globalization: The Human Consequences* (p. 4). London: Polity.

Silva, D. (2009). Internet Has Only Just Begun, Say Founders. *Phys.Org*, April 22. Retrieved from https://phys.org/news/2009-04-internet-begun-founders.html. Accessed on August 1, 2017.

FURTHER READING

Birkinbine, B., Gomez, R., & Wasko, J. (Eds.). (2016). *Global media giants*. New York, NY: Routledge.

Bratton, B. H. (2016). *The stack: On software and sovereignty*. Cambridge: MIT Press.

Deibert, R. J. (2013). *Black code: Surveillance, privacy, and the dark side of the internet*. Toronto: Signal.

Engler, M., & Engler, P. *This is an uprising: How nonviolent revolt is shaping the twenty-first century*. New York, NY: Nation Books.

Ford, M. (2015). *Rise of the robots: Technology and the threat of mass unemployment*. New York, NY: Basic Books.

Frase, P. (2016). *Four futures: Life after capitalism*. London: Verso.

Golumbia, D. (2016). *The politics of bitcoin: Software as right-wing extremism*. Minneapolis, MI: University of Minnesota Press.

Gusterson, H. (2016). *Drones: Remote control warfare*. Cambridge: MIT Press.

Lynch, M. P. (2016). *The Internet of us: Knowing more and understanding less in the age of big data*. New York, NY: Liveright Press.

Mason, P. (2016). *Postcapitalism: A guide to our future.*
New York, NY: Farrar, Straus and Giroux.

Maxwell, R., & Miller, T. (2012). *Greening the media.*
New York, NY: Oxford.

Pasquale, F. (2016). *The black box society: The
secret algorithms that control money and information.*
Cambridge, MA: Harvard University Press.

Qiu, J. L. (2016). *Goodbye iSlave.* Urbana, IL: University of
Illinois Press.

Rose, D. (2014). *Enchanted objects: Innovation, design, and
the future of technology.* New York, NY: Scribner.

Sax, D. (2016). *The revenge of analog: Real things and why
they matter.* New York, NY: PublicAffairs.

Taplin, J. (2017). *Move fast and break things: How
Facebook, Google, and Amazon cornered culture and
undermined democracy.* New York, NY: Little, Brown and
Company.

Taylor, A. (2014). *The people's platform: Taking back power
and culture in the digital age.* Toronto: Random House.

Tufekci, Z. (2017). *Twitter and tear gas: The power and fra-
gility of networked protest.* New Haven, CT: Yale University
Press.

Turkle, S. (2015). *Reclaiming conversation: The power of
talk in a digital age.* New York, NY: Penguin Press.

Wu, T. (2016). *The attention merchants: The epic scramble
to get inside our heads.* New York, NY: Knopf.

INDEX

Adobe, 71
*The Age of Spiritual
  Machines* (Kurzweil),
  123
Airbnb, 71
Algorithms, 12, 139
Alibaba, 86–87
AliCloud, 86
Alphabet, 67
Amazon, 3, 5, 6, 18, 19,
  21, 22, 27, 29, 44, 70,
  71, 72, 86, 107, 111,
  132
Amazon Machine Learning
  (AML), 46
Amazon Wallet, 76
Amazon Web Services, 8,
  18, 30, 68, 72, 73
AMC Theatres, 90
American Big Tech, 65–76
Apple, 2, 5, 11, 18, 22, 27,
  44, 66, 67, 68, 69, 76,
  78, 103, 107, 132
Apple Music subscription
  service, 66
Apple Watch, 41
Artificial Intelligence (AI),
  121, 171

AT&T, 61, 63, 107, 182,
  183, 185
Automation and jobs,
  168–170
Azure, 68, 105

Baidu, 87
Barclays, 85
Basic income, 207–208
Bell Atlantic, 79
Belt and Road, 92
Berners-Lee, Tim, 1, 175
Big Data Analytics, 4, 5, 8,
  9, 14, 28, 33, 57, 66,
  71, 82, 83, 101
Big Five, 66, 74
Big Tech, 65–76
Bing, 3
Bio-chip, 99
Bio-hacking firm
  BioNyfiken, 99
Bitcoin, 191
Blackberry, 27
Body cameras, 147
"Bro" culture, 134

Cambridge Analytica, 140
Capital One, 71

Central Intelligence Agency
    (CIA), 20, 43, 71, 84
Children, 114–115
China, 86–96
China, American
    companies in, 91
China Mobile, 89
China Telecom, 89, 91
China Unicom, 89
Chinese historical
    imaginary, 92
Chrome, 3
CIA. *See* The Central
    Intelligence Agency
    (CIA)
Cisco, 22, 45, 80
Citizenship, 194–195
Climate change, 176
Cloud Computing, 4, 5, 6,
    9, 14, 16–28, 24, 68,
    70, 82, 83, 133
Code.org, 69
Cold War, 7
Coltan mines, 74
Commercial Internet,
    origins, 59–64
Commercialism
 and commodification,
    132
 and concentration,
    130–141
Commodified self, 102
Commodify, 100–106
Convergence, power and
    peril of, 51–55
Criminal hacking, 159
Cryptocurrency, 191
Cultural studies, 5

Cyber-technologies, 121
Cyber warfare, 141–148

Dark Web, 3–4
Dataism, 121
Deep Web, 3–4
Defense Advanced
    Research Projects
    Agency (DARPA), 59
Defense of Marriage Act,
    180
Demography, 100–106
Digital communication
    networks, 60
Digital computer-to-
    computer
    communication
    systems, 61
Digital positivism, 30
Digital world, 3
Drones, 147
DuoSkin, 97

E-commerce business, 70
Edge Computing, 25
Electoral College victory, 35
Electronic
    communication, 2
Emergency medical
    services, 147
Environmental impact,
    148–156
Environmental Protection
    Agency, 176
E-pollution, 199–201
Ericsson, 27
European Union, 195
E-waste, 148

Facebook, 3, 5, 18, 21, 27, 44, 73, 76, 78, 111, 132
Fake news, 139
Federal Communications Commission, 61
Feudalism, 15
Firefox, 3
Fire services, 147
5G wireless, 88, 89
Fiverr, 113–114
Fortune (magazine), 109
Foxconn, 75
Frankenstein (Shelley, Mary), 124

Gartner, 30, 169
GE Capital, 77
General Electric (GE), 45, 48, 49, 71, 86, 93, 124
Gig economy, 111
Global Positioning System (GPS), 147
Gmail, 3, 18, 67, 69
Google, 2, 5, 6, 11, 18, 21, 27, 28, 44, 68, 69, 76, 85, 111, 132, 196
Google News, 67
GPS. *See* Global Positioning System (GPS)
Great Depression, 182

Hewlett-Packard, 78, 80
Hollywood, 88
Homeland and border security, 147
HSBC, 85

Huawei, 89
Hybrid Cloud, 24

IBM, 27, 45, 61, 79, 90
iCloud, 3, 18, 66
Information Management: A Proposal (Berners-Lee, Tim), 1
Instagram, 3, 73
International Monetary Fund, 34
International Telecommunication Union, 63
Internet-based devices, 9
Internet communication, 1–2
Internet-enabled consumer devices, 50
Internet of hackable things, 156–167
Internet of Things, 4, 5, 6, 7, 9, 12, 13, 14, 39–51
Inter-networking, 60
iPhone, 74
Iron Triangle, 75
iTunes, 134

Lethal Autonomous Weapons Systems, 83
LG, 162
Lloyds Bank, 85
Lyft, 112–113

Mechanical Turk, 111
Media Lab, 98
Metaphor, 115–117

Microsoft, 5, 18, 22, 27,
    44, 69, 107, 110, 132
Militarism, 197–199
Monbiot, George, 39
Myth, 117–120

National Association of
    Broadcasters, 131
National Science
    Foundation (NSF), 60
National Security Agency
    (NSA), 20, 43, 84, 145
Network Neutrality, 186
New Silk Road, 92
New Yorker (magazine), 2,
    17
New York Times, 178
Next Internet, 58, 64, 127
Next Internet, government
    embraces the, 82–85
Nixon Administration, 176
Nokia, 27
Nordstrom Rack store, 30
Nortel, 27

O2, 85
Oracle, 80
Origin of Species, 32

Panoptic sort, 104
Parkhill, Douglas,
    209–210
Patriot Act, 22
Pay-for-storage service, 66
Pinterest, 71
Playbour, 108
Political economy, 5
Post-internet world

Big Five, 193–195
control e-pollution,
    199–201
despair and disruption,
    175–177
historical imagination,
    181–187
human right, basic
    income, 204–208
impossible dreams,
    180–181
public utility in
    communication,
    208–212
regulate commercialism,
    195–197
resist militarism, 197–199
restore privacy, 202–204
revenge of analog,
    177–180
Post-Internet world, 2
Precision agriculture, 31
Privacy, 156–167,
    202–204
Private Cloud, 23
Public Cloud, 23, 66
Public utility model,
    13–14, 186–187,
    208–212

QQ, 88
Quantified self, 101
Quine, Willard Van
    Orman, 4

Rackspace, 28
Reclaiming Conversation
    (Turkle, Sherry), 179

The Revenge of Analog
    (Sax, David), 178
Robot, 126–127
Royal Bank of Scotland, 85

Safari, 3
Salesforce.com, 8, 23, 27
Samsung, 74, 162
Siemens, 27
Silicon Valley, 2, 27, 88, 121
Singularity, 120–121
Sky, 85
Smart cities, 32
Snapchat, 3, 107
Snowden, Edward, 31
Social media, 3
Social movements, 187–191
Society and technology,
    15–16
Solutionism, 36
Sony, 162
Sublime, 126
Surveillance, 156–167
Surveillance capitalism, 161
Surveillance state, 161

TCP/IP Internet standard, 63
Tech aristocracy, 110
Technology
  and power, 57–58
  and society, 15–16
Tencent, 88
To the Cloud, 4
Twitter, 3, 80, 107

Uber, 112
Ubiquitous computing,
    55–56

United States Cyber
    Command, 3
United States Postal
    Service, 181, 186
Uptime Legal Systems, 23

Verizon, 53, 79
Verizon's Yahoo, 3
Videotex, 26
Vodafone, 85

Wanda Group, 89
Washington Post
    (newspaper), 72
Watson, 90
Wearable sensors, 147
Web of problems, 6
Web-Pay, 76
WeChat, 88
WhatsApp, 73, 185
Wi-Fi-enabled devices, 13
Wi-Fi-enabled
    thermostats, 9
Wi-Fi systems, 46
WikiLeaks data, 31
Wikipedia, 87
Williams, Raymond, 5
Wired (magazine), 29, 137
Worker commodity,
    106–114
World Economic Forum,
    27
World Trade Organization,
    94
World Wide Web, 1

Yahoo, 79
YouTube, 67

Printed in the United States
By Bookmasters